NEWMAN AT LITTLEMORE

Newman at Littlemore

Bernard Basset, SJ

Gracewing

This edition first published in England in 2019 by Gracewing
2 Southern Avenue
Leominster
Herefordshire
HR6 0QF
United Kingdom
www.gracewing.co.uk

ISBN 978 085244 942 4

Typeset by Gracewing

Cover design by Bernardita Peña Hurtado
Drawing by Carrie Jones

CONTENTS

Contents...v

Foreword...vii

1 A New Vicar at St Mary's...1

    Littlemore—the lost village—three miles from St Mary's, its Church...3

    The Village he loved..6

    Newman at Oriel..7

    St Mary's...11

    First years in Littlemore......................................14

    Mrs Newman arrives...17

2 A Church for Littlemore 25

    Dedication...28

    Bloxam Arrives 29

    'I am tempted to pitch my tent here'....................31

        Littlemore. April 18th 1840.............................37

    This is a Secret...38

    My Books are on the move....................................41

3 The College 47

    First Description of the College.............................49

    The Press get it wrong...50

    The First Arrivals...51

    Lockhart..56

    Lockhart leaves...59

Last Oxford Sermon...60

The Parting of Friends..61

The Temporary Oratory...62

The Oratory...64

1844–45...65

The Development of Doctrine...66

The End of the College..68

4 The Final Step...71

John Henry's Reception...71

Letters to Mrs Bowden, Oct 8th 1845....................................72

Epilogue...76

5 The College Today..79

Part I...79

Part II...83

Appendix..91

Three letters of John Henry Newman connected with
Littlemore..91

Letter to his sister Jemima Mozley, 22nd March 1845...........91

Letter to his sister Jemima Mozley, 8th October 1845.............94

Letter to Revd George William Huntingford, 17th June 1868.....95

FOREWORD

F R BERNARD BASSET'S *Newman at Littlemore* has been a source of knowledge and inspiration for countless Newman friends since it was first published in 1983. Fr Basset lived at the College in his retirement and so brought personal detailed knowledge and experience of the College to his readers. His witty style increases the pleasure with which one makes acquaintance with John Henry's friends, family and parishioners. The illustrations help us to form a picture of Newman's Oxford which played such an influential part in the life and thinking of this 'eminent Victorian'. It was especially at Littlemore that Newman, in the words of Pope St Paul VI, 'guided solely by love of the truth and fidelity to Christ, traced an itinerary, the most toilsome but also the greatest, the most meaningful, the most conclusive, that human thought ever travelled during the nineteenth century indeed one might say during the modern era, to arrive at the fullness of truth'.

I am pleased that Gracewing have undertaken to republish this valuable work. Since 1986 the Spiritual Family the Work have taken care of The College with great love and devotion. Under their auspices it has developed into a place of pilgrimage for Newman friends from around the world. This new edition of *Newman at Littlemore* has been edited and enlarged by the Community of the Work and for this pilgrims to Littlemore will be grateful.

✠ Robert Byrne
Bishop of Hexham and Newcastle

1 A NEW VICAR AT ST MARY'S

I N THE UNIVERSITY world, promotions and resigna-
tions prove effective in adding change to the staid,
academic scene. Thus, in the Fall of 1827, Oriel
College, Oxford, suffered one such upheaval when Dr
Edward Copleston, the distinguished Provost, was named
Bishop of Llandaff. The new bishop, we are told, tried his
new outfit at Church next Sunday, but wore his wig the
wrong way round.

Dr Copleston gone, a new Provost had to be elected. A
tense campaign between supporters of John Keble and
Edward Hawkins finally put Hawkins in the driving seat.
As Hawkins at the time was Vicar of St Mary's, the fellows
of Oriel had to vote again. The founder of Oriel had built
St Mary's in the middle ages and the College retained the
rights of a lay patron, presenting a candidate to the bishop
for the vacant post. The cleric thus selected noted the
occasion in his private journal; 'Friday, March 14th;
instituted by the Bishop of Oxford to St Mary's. Thursday,
March 28th 1828; inducted into St Mary's by Buckley of
Merton; baptised Norris' child, George Edward and
churched Mrs N.'

In this unassuming way, Victorian history, even Church
history, was changed. The new Vicar of St Mary's, the Revd
John Henry Newman, aged twenty-seven, was, at the time,
of no importance; little known outside his college and of
no great significance within. His shyness derived from a
variety of causes of which we may mention four. Educated
at a very good private School in Ealing, he lacked the social
contacts of those from more famous Public Schools.
Again, though his salary as a fellow was adequate, he was

partly supporting his recently widowed mother by meeting his younger brother's college fees. Further, though undoubtedly clever—a fellowship at Oriel College was, at that time, the highest of all honours—he had botched his Finals at The Schools. In the jargon of the day, he expressed his feelings neatly 'It was very great impartiality on their part to take so despicable a thing as an Under-the-Line, merely because they liked his examination best.'

The fourth reason for his shyness—if this is the right word—was the new Vicar's piety. His background was evangelical, his theology Calvinist, though both these traits were mellowing. Two of his greatest friends shunned him, at first, for this. In his undergraduate days, his rigid attitude to alcohol did not endear him to the majority of students who drank too much. In this sphere, too, he was thawing; from temperament, rather than for any theological scruples; the new Vicar managed no great interest in sport. His secular relaxation lay in music and you do not go far in college if you play no more than a violin. The new Vicar was rarely unhappy but as he put it later 'During the first years of my residence at Oriel, though proud of my college, I was not at home there. I was very much alone and I used often to take my daily walk by myself.'

When John Henry Newman was appointed Vicar of St Mary's, he had no great reputation as a preacher and little experience of pastoral life. He had, however, a craving, a determination; as soon as he was ordained a deacon on June 13th 1824, he accepted an appointment at St Clement's parish, just across Magdalen bridge. He wrote to his father: 'I am convinced it is necessary to get used to parochial duties early, and that a fellow of a College, after ten years residence in Oxford, feels very awkward among the poor and ignorant.' No such aloofness is seen in Newman's life. Though he only worked in St Clement's for less than two years, with a Vicar who was over eighty, he visited every house in his district and kept a precise list. He raised the money for a larger church and was particularly kindly to Sectarians. He was, I think, sad when his contract finished and added work in College, forced him to withdraw.

The old church of St Clement's

When John Henry Newman was made Vicar of St Mary's, he wrote 'I preached my first University sermon … it was to me like the feeling of spring weather after winter, and, if I may so speak, I came out of my shell.'

Littlemore—the lost village—three miles from St Mary's, its Church

In a booklet entitled *Newman at Littlemore*, Vicar and village must be brought together before our Pilgrim's Progress may begin. This happened more quickly than expected, for, on the very day of his induction to St Mary's, after lunch with Thomas Arnold, the new Vicar and the Provost set off for Littlemore. Some attention should be given to the journey, for Newman would cover the road—three miles each way—many times a week for eighteen years.

The population of Oxford had already swept across the river to St Clement's parish, in which Newman had served as deacon and in which the first Catholic chapel, named after St Ignatius, lay hid. Once through St Clement's, various paths led up the hill and across the fields. The choristers of Magdalen College chose the field paths on their annual outings, where the Reverend Edward Abbott, a visitor, 'went along the river bank by a broad footpath' with hedges right down to the water and two weirs on the way. The one official road, crossing the Cowley marshes and heading for Henley was used by the coaches and farmers' carts.

Over his eighteen years of moving up and down, Newman took a fly on occasions when he had luggage, but such transport was not cheap. In the early years, he sometimes rode and for a spell had a horse of his own called Klepper, a mare described as 'a pretty creature with Arab blood'. Newman enjoyed riding, but Klepper once unseated him near Brighton, causing him to break his glasses and cut his nose. One other accident—a tragic one—befell him near Littlemore. He and his friend Dornford were going at *an ordinary road trot* when the horses of a passing wagon took fright and the wagonner, Thomas Wing, was killed. Friends would later recall how Newman would always step out to protest if he saw wagon horses with no-one at their heads.

In the main, Newman walked to and from Littlemore, preparing his sermons and calling in on parishioners along the way. We have two accounts from undergraduates who saw him. One writes 'I met Newman almost daily, striding along the Oxford Road, with large head, prominent nose, tortoiseshell spectacles, emaciated but ruddy face, spare figure, whose leanness was exaggerated by the close-fitting tail-coat then worn.' William Lockhart wrote, fifty years later, how a companion pointed out Newman to him:

> I looked and, then, I saw him passing along in his characteristic way, walking fast, without any dignity of gait but earnest, like one who had a purpose; yet so humble and self-forgetting in every portion of his external appearance, that you would not have thought him, at first sight, a man remarkable for anything.

Newman by Mary Giberne

The Village he loved

As you might expect, official guide books give a too rosy picture and make Littlemore better than it was. Thus *The History, Gazetteer and Directory of the County of Oxford* (1852) describes the village of Littlemore as neat and rural, three miles south south-east from Oxford and tells us that in the parish 'before the time of King Henry II, there was a Benedictine nunnery, now in ruins called The Minchery.' The Gazetteer was published six years after the Vicar had left the village for good. He never knew the development which the Gazetteer proudly mentions, the Pauper Lunatic Asylum, opened in 1851 'to which 114 persons were admitted last year'. It is pleasing to report, more than a century later, that Littlemore now boasts one of the finest Psychiatric Hospitals in the country and that The Minchery has been beautifully restored.

When the new Vicar first arrived, he found much to depress him; he told the bishop later that there was one straggling street and 'scarcely a house beyond the rank of cottage in the village'; that Littlemore had neither Church nor school. Later, in his famous *Apologia*, he would use Littlemore as an example of parochial muddle, 'it lies in three, perhaps in four distinct parishes, so that, of particular houses, it is difficult to say whether they are in St Mary's Oxford, or in Cowley, or in Iffley, or in Sandford; the line of demarcation running even through them'. Littlemore was a sad and dying village, the population fell from 452 residents to 194 in Newman's first ten years. Those who belonged to St Mary's parish were supposed to walk three miles to church on Sundays just as their Vicar faced three miles each way to visit them. The village had three or four fine stone houses, three or four inns, three or four forges and, of course, the village stocks.

Yet, despite such discouragements, John Henry Newman secretly loved the little village and expressed this affection to his friends. In the very first year, he wrote to his sister Harriett:

> My ride of a morning is generally solitary, but I almost prefer to be alone. When the spirits are good, everything is delightful in the view of still nature which the country gives, I have learned to like dying trees and black meadows—swamps have their grace and fogs their sweetness. Oh for some small cure of a few hundreds a year and no preferment as this world calls it. But you know that this is wishing for idleness and I do not think that I shall have this obscurity because I wish for it.

The George

Newman at Oriel

Her brother was telling the truth when he shared with Harriett his longing for a little parish away from the busy world. Such a craving for solitude in a quiet domestic setting would remain with him throughout his life. Yet his guess that such obscurity was unlikely also proved correct.

Though he was among the most single-minded of men, he was the victim of a system which made him at once an Academic figure of distinction and a simple parish priest.

The Richmond portrait of Newman

His parishioners at Littlemore knew nothing of their vicar's life in Oxford, while the dons at his College cared little about his work in Littlemore. To bridge this gap, we should spend a paragraph or two at Oriel College and at St Mary's Church, across the High Street, before returning to Littlemore.

It would be an impertinence to attempt a sketch of John Henry's life in College; countless excellent accounts already cover his progress step by step. Sufficient it is to note, that in College, John Henry Newman was not his own master; though he held in turn the posts of tutor, treasurer, dean and bursar—transient and time-consuming offices. He occupied the same quarters—first floor near the chapel—for some fifteen years. John Henry did not smoke, came to enjoy wine later, played a part in introducing the Common Room to tea. He had many intimate friends and, perhaps, as many adversaries among his contemporaries. Years later, he would quote with approval a remark made about him: 'Here is a man who, when he is silent will never begin to speak and when he once begins to speak will never stop'.

Photographs are commonplace today. In Newman's college years, the camera still had teething troubles, but two portraits by distinguished artists more than supply our needs. In 1844 George Richmond produced his famous drawing, greatly appreciated and frequently displayed. Two intimate friends, however, did not like it and Henry Wilberforce wrote to Newman 'The likeness is no doubt diminished by not having your glasses, which seem to me almost a necessary part of you'. In the following year, Sir William Ross painted the portrait, now in Keble College and the miniature which hangs in Newman's room at Littlemore. We see John Henry full face and with his spectacles. As he sums us up through his thick lenses, we may note the calm determination which made Hawkins and many others fear him but drew many young disciples to Littlemore.

If two great artists could vary so much in their impressions of Newman, we may have to check our attitudes. Though he was a genius, he was not a great scholar in the Academic sense. His was the brilliance of a great barrister or journalist. His two novels excepted—John Henry wrote only two books, without a specific occasion, in a lifetime; his other innumerable volumes were collections of sermons, tracts, articles and letters, written for a purpose in the present moment, often under pressure and against the clock. At Oriel, he began with an article for an Encyclopedia, next, became a powerful contributor in many journals, especially *The British Magazine* (High Church) and *The British Critic* (Tractarian). When we return with him to Littlemore, we must not forget these commitments and, of course, the publication of the Tracts.

With the start of the Tractarian Movement, impressions of John Henry Newman need a further change. Tracts had been as common as dirt for centuries and the small group of clergymen who met at Hadleigh in 1833 had no thought of using them. Newman, who joined the group a little later, despite some opposition, took the initiative in this. He planned the title Tracts for the Times and engineered a further title 'The Oxford Movement'; Oxford meant Oriel for him. He was sincere in his protests that he was no leader, in his praise of Keble, Pusey and others but the brain behind the Tracts was his. Unofficially, he was editor and censor and dashed off the first seven Tracts himself. His was the decision to make the Tracts anonymous and he gave as his reason 'You may say things worth saying in themselves but not fit for you to say'. His, too, was the note of challenge, the slogan in Tract One, '*Choose your side, since side you shortly must*'.

The Tracts covered every aspect of Church life. Newman himself wrote more than thirty, the early ones selling for a penny and usually short. A Master of English prose, he managed in his tracts the pungency and punch of a top-class journalist All his tracts were and still are informative, some were deeply spiritual, not a few challenging, with a many a thwack at the Pope. Still more astonishing, from his humble rooms in Oriel, he bargained with publishers, rallied the clergy to organize distribution throughout England, mounted his horse, on occasion, to ferry the tracts to the Oxfordshire countryside. Money became a problem but John Henry had skill, even in that department. By the time he had reached Tract 90, the operation had more than paid its way.

St Mary's

On our way to Littlemore, we should, I think, pause for a moment at St Mary's, a few hundred yards from Oriel, at the end of Magpie Lane. The history of this great University Church need not detain us nor need we consider John Henry Newman's myriad activities as Vicar of the parish for fifteen years. Instead, we hurry to the pulpit, recalling his statement 'It was at Oxford and by my parochial sermons, that I gained my influence'. He preached his first sermon at St Mary's in March 1828 and we read in his private journal 'I preached No. 604, my last sermon, September 25th 1843.'

John Henry was as surprised as his College authorities at his success. He was not chosen to follow Edward Hawkins as Vicar for his eloquence. His earlier sermons at St Clement's and elsewhere passed unnoticed, though they were most carefully prepared. His mother and sisters read his early sermons and were delighted, as one would expect. As far as we know, John Henry had no training as a preacher. Dr Hawkins was to play an important part in weaning him away from the heavily evangelical doctrines of his early sermons. John Henry also recalls 'Dr Hawkins, further, taught me to weigh my words and to be cautious in my statements … and he used to snub me severely on reading, as he was kind enough to do, the first sermons that I wrote'.

St Mary's, Oxford

As a young clergyman, John Henry had his troubles in the pulpit, as he explained in a letter to a colleague who wrote for help. He replied 'If it is any comfort to you so to say, I have, before now, felt in my own mind the distress you speak of about the right mode of preaching—at one time (as you may have heard me say) so sorely that I must have given up my curacy, nay have left the Church, I cannot doubt you are perfectly safe under Our Lord's teaching waiting on Him, day by day'. Elsewhere Newman mentioned two other helpful tips. He found it easier to prepare each sermon with one particular listener in mind and, in an early tract, he reminds the preacher that he is not in the pulpit just to please the people, but to lead them, as St Paul commands 'How can we hold fast the form of sound words and keep that which is committed to our trust if our influence is to depend simply on our popularity?'

The comments from the hundreds who flocked to Newman's sermons are far too many to be mentioned here. Three may suffice to illustrate the effectiveness of his rules, above-mentioned. The future Principal Shairp wrote 'He laid his finger—how gently yet how powerfully— on some inner place in the hearer's heart and told him things about himself he had never known till then'. J.A. Froude, the eminent historian, put it this way 'he seemed to be addressing the most sacred consciousness of each of us—as the eyes of a portrait appear to look at every person in the room'. The future Father Faber, in a letter of 1836, paid striking tribute to the preacher in an instant resolution 'Under God's grace, I will raise my structure of love upon a solid groundwork of holy fear.' Newman could be very severe, with the voice of conscience as a recurring theme. Yet there was no blood and thunder in his sermons, few gestures, no histrionics and no Parson's voice. Those who have read the Parochial and Plain sermons in the last hundred and fifty years may agree with the verdict of a young scholar that Newman came down to St Mary's each Sunday to put before them truths about which he had prayed through the week.

Young Oxford's tribute to John Henry is more impressive when his role as Vicar of St Mary's is more fully understood. The great church catered for two distinct congregations, popularly known as Town and Gown. Each Sunday in term time, undergraduates and dons could attend their College chapels or escort the Vice-Chancellor

to the University Church. Special University preachers
were selected for the official occasion, and were appointed
for two years.

The Vicar of St Mary's had a humbler role, for his duties
were confined to the townsfolk; he visited the sick,
instructed the children and, at 5.00 p.m., on Sundays
provided Evensong for the relatively few residents, shop-
keepers, servants and visitors. In his earlier years, and
during University vacations, John Henry preached to a half
empty church. Such a situation did not endure for long.
Little by little, undergraduates, graduates and visitors
either went to church twice or cut the University's selected
preacher, to hear the Vicar in the afternoon. Eyewitnesses
put the crowd at as many as five hundred and Lord
Coleridge sums it up 'There was scarcely a man of note in
the University, old or young, who did not, during the last
two or three years of Newman's incumbency, habitually
attend the service and listen to the sermons.' Friction, in
these final years, was great. Newman's adversaries in the
college could not stop him or deprive him of office, for he
owed his position to the bishop and was protected by
Canon Law. Some Heads of Colleges changed the time of
dinner but to no avail.

First years in Littlemore

For the new Vicar, the hamlet of Littlemore, on the fringe
of his parish, became at once a challenge, a duty and a rest.
As a deacon John Henry had called on every parishioner
in St Clement's, street by street. Littlemore only had one
street. There were, however, scattered cottages in plenty
and new houses under construction on Rose Hill. Not a
moment could be lost. When his widowed mother begged
him to visit her in Brighton, he answered 'As for leaving
my church for the time you name, it is quite impossible.

The long vacation is the only time I can have for knowing anything about Littlemore.' On May 9th 1828 he entered in his journal 'Walked with Pusey and W to Littlemore—called on Mrs Birmingham—began sermon Number 165.'

It is a pleasure to mention Mrs Birmingham as one of the first of his Littlemore friends. Her little girl was ill. The new Vicar called several times to see the sick child and even went to the Infirmary, when he heard that she was there. Indeed it was the children who led him to their parents; one entry in his journal finds him examining Maria Martin, Edwin Mills, Smith's daughter and Greening's daughter for confirmation, while poor little Frederic William Varney, through a slip of the pen, we hope, was buried on July 11th and baptised on July 13th.

In these early days, the Vicar's journal, with its tangle of initials, abbreviations and jottings is as daunting as a jigsaw puzzle but supplies a perfect picture, when all the pieces are in place. Three themes are constant, week after week. John Henry is working daily on his sermons, each is numbered, but the system of numbering is not plain. Next, he records the books he is reading—he was, we know, working systematically through the writings of the early Fathers—so St Ignatius of Antioch or St Polycarp turn up suddenly, among the Littlemore parishioners. Thirdly, Littlemore features regularly and his problems are great.

Almost as soon as he was appointed Vicar, John Henry decided that Littlemore needed its own Church. He raised the matter at the next College Audit and invited his two friends and fellow tutors at Oriel, Hurrell Froude and Robert Wilberforce to co-operate in his scheme. He worded it this way:

> My plan is this—ultimately to make Littlemore and
> St Mary's practically separate parishes and, at
> present, provide a person who would take Littlemore

entirely, or almost entirely, to himself, having nothing
to do with St Mary's.

He expected a refusal and received one but he had to
present a plan. As Littlemore was so poor, it could ill
support a pastor but John Henry always looked far ahead.
Further, in the two years since he had been weaned from
Calvinism, he no longer saw pastoral efforts as sufficient;
the faithful needed a church as a permanent sacramental
reminder of God's presence in their midst John Henry was
never a ritualist but his interest in church architecture
proved enduring and extended from the chapel in Trinity
College, Oxford, to the great cathedral in Milan.

For his church in Littlemore he had to wait seven years.
To the shortage of money was added the hostility of neighbouring parishes who could charge double fees for non-
parishioners. Of the clerk at Iffley it was said 'he is equally
opposed to the innovation; in the first place he has buried
half the parish and he did hope to bury the other half and
besides, he will lose double fees.' John Henry could suggest
a further obstacle. As he first expressed it: 'the Provost has
negatived my proposition for doing something for Littlemore' and he added later 'I think I am right in saying that the
Provost steadily threw cold water on the building.'

The new Vicar had no option and his first task was to
find a room. Certain dissenters had already established a
meeting-house in the village and, with their parish church
three miles away in Oxford, one could hardly blame
Church of England villagers who welcomed such an
exchange. Others, more loyal, made their way to the parish
churches of Cowley, Sandford, Iffley, and the less interested, stayed away. John Henry, as Vicar of Littlemore,
buried a boy in Cowley and officiated at the marriage of
his own sister in Iffley Church. In his journal, he mentions
distributing tickets to the children for the Confirmation

service and, if the guess is right, here was a unique occasion when the villagers from Littlemore went three miles to their parish church.

John Henry eventually found a room. Mrs Birmingham first lent him one in her house, later, we find him settling a bill with a Mr Waring and asking that his chair should be moved further from the door. No traces or records of these first meeting-houses now survive. All that we now have is a record of his decision to hold a weekly meeting and a letter to his sister Jemima, (Oriel College, Febr. 8th 1829) 'I began my Littlemore evening catechetical lecture last Sunday. I am now returned about an hour from it and am not fatigued'.

Mrs Newman arrives

The Newman family. A drawing of around 1830

Mrs Newman, a widow, was nearing sixty when she came
to Littlemore. The failure of her husband's bank had left
him bankrupt and she supported her family on her marriage
jointure which some experts reckon at £5,000. Poor Mr
Newman paid all his debts and bore his humiliation with
resignation; we may meet all the family round his deathbed
on September 29th 1824. At the time, John Henry was a
deacon at St Clement's; he notes in his journal 'Francis,
Jemima and Mary came to town. Charles and I sat up till
four o'clock; my Mother, Francis and Harriett, all night'.
Later he added of his dead father 'on Thursday he looked
beautiful, such calmness, sweetness, composure and
majesty were in his countenance. Can a man be a materialist
who sees a dead body? I had never seen one before'.

Her husband gone, Mrs Newman and her three daugh-
ters, stayed near London for a while and, then, settled in
Brighton in the fading decade of the Regency age. Two of
her three sons were still in training and John Henry, her
eldest was her pride and joy. She wrote to him in 1830 'You
know that, like yourself, I am no flatterer . . . but you were
the silent pride of my early life and now I look to you as
the guide and comforter of my age.'

When Mrs Newman penned this, she had already
recovered from a further disaster; her youngest, Mary, aged
nineteen, was taken ill on Jan 4th 1828 at evening dinner
and died on the following day. John Henry, who was in
Brighton at the time, took months, even years, to master
his sorrow, whereas his mother soon settled down to her
routine. She was a simple, middle-class mother, partial to
gossip, devoted to all her children though Charles and
Francis annoyed her 'for they consider that they alone see
things right.' Of Huguenot descent, Mrs Newman was, in
every day terms, a devout, Low Church, Protestant. Two
themes run through all her letters to John Henry, first that

she does not want to be a nuisance, next that she must thank God for great blessings received. After her husband's death, she cherished two secret desires, that her children would marry and that she could be near her eldest son.

John Henry never spoke to her or to anyone about marriage; she had died long before he clearly expressed his views on paper, in his novel *Loss and Gain* and in the *Apologia*. He felt called to remain celibate. He was to her a very dutiful son, wrote to her frequently and rode down to Brighton on occasion, but he was impossibly busy in Oxford with his weekly sermons, his articles, his parish, which included Littlemore. Once when she complained of not hearing from him, he replied tartly 'I have written you five letters in twelve days.' Again, when she hinted at coming to Oxford, he replied in a letter to Jemima 'Indeed, to speak frankly, it would annoy me much to find you near here.'

This brusque response was justified for John Henry had planned a delightful holiday for his mother and sisters in the long vacation, renting a house in the quaint little village of Horspath, near Littlemore. This was a common practice in the University. A tutor, or coach, would collect a small party of earnest students for a working holiday. After the stay at Horspath, John Henry moved to Nuneham Courtney, another lovely village, in which his friend Dornford had a cottage which was not engaged. For two or three months, John Henry's routine was changed. Now he slept in the village and rode into Oxford of a morning and visited his parishioners at Littlemore when riding back to Horspath or Nuneham Courtney at night. Jemima, Harriett and Mrs Newman met John Henry's friends, attended various University functions and, in the evenings, at the cottages, enjoyed many recitals; John Henry and Blanco White bringing their violins.

Mrs Newman and the girls eventually went back to Brighton but not for long. Mrs, Newman could not settle down away from Oxford. John Henry had misgivings and he once expressed the fear that by coming to live closer, his mother might in fact see him less. Perhaps through Frank, Mrs Newman heard of a cottage available near Iffley and John Henry eventually gave way. Three or four times a week, he walked to Iffley with friends to inspect the cottage, to buy new furniture and he adds 'I took very great pains to make the cottage comfortable.' Mrs Newman arrived on October 22nd 1830 and wrote to her son that evening 'We all like Iffley... and I am much pleased at being so near to Littlemore. I shall be delighted if you can make us useful according to our abilities. I assure you, I shall come with a willing heart.'

Mrs Newman first settled at Rosehill. Two ancient cottages had been joined together—a common experiment—which enabled her to cater for her son. Harriett put it this way 'John has now taken possession of his new compartment—consisting of a hall, staircase, study and bedroom—quite grand is he not? His study is very pretty and comfortable for summer. We have made a new large window in it, allowing him a view of our garden and a very pleasant lookout towards Oxford. He is very much charmed.' In a sense, Mrs Newman's house became John Henry's first vicarage. As he told the bishop 'A portion of St Mary's parish lies in the hamlet of Littlemore ... Part of the year I have been residing, not in Oxford but close upon this portion (there being no house belonging to me or suitable within it). I am in the practice of having a weekly lecture in Littlemore throughout the year.'

For two years, John Henry had a choice; he could sleep in Oriel and walk or ride to Iffley or sleep at Iffley and walk or ride to Oxford every day. On Sunday, December 2nd

1832, he was the select preacher at St Mary's; he preached on the Wilfulness of Saul and his sister, Harriett, who heard him, remarked that he was leaving Oxford 'with a sting in your tail'. John Henry left Oxford the next day, collecting his mail from Rosehill on the way. He was off with Archdeacon Froude and Hurrell for his first visit to the Continent.

Six months later, John Henry reached his Mother's house at Iffley on July 9th 1833. His continental tour, so vital to his story, is not directly concerned with Littlemore. That he had come face to face with Rome and disapproved; face to face with death from fever in a remote Sicilian village, affected Littlemore only because he brought back the words of his most famous hymn, *Lead Kindly Light*, composed on his travels and a wig to hide a temporary loss of hair.

His Mother had moved house and now lived at Rose Bank, further down the hill and with a larger garden and from here she, with Harriett and Jemima, played a more active part in Littlemore life. The girls gathered the children together and ran a rudimentary school. The old and the sick were visited and, even more important, the first efforts were made to raise money for the church.

A visitor to Rose Bank wrote in a letter

> They have already got £300 and have not begun the regular subscription yet. Mr Newman means to refuse money from unworthy persons; for instance, from one who is expected to offer to give, though he never goes to church. There is to be a sermon in St Mary's in a week or two, in which he means to exhort everybody 'to give large sums' but he means to say that people may either give at the door or the Bank, in order that nobody may give unwillingly or from shame, as he does not wish for money given from unworthy motives. I particularly

enjoy hearing his grave authoritative way of expressing his feelings and intentions.

In April 1835, the Newman girls presented their brother with a petition to Oriel 'We send you the petition and heartily wish it success, and you as little plague as possible.' *All* the St Mary's householders (sixty-two or sixty-three) but one who is not to be found. Everyone is full of hope and anxiety. One man said 'If he could but live to be buried in Littlemore churchyard, he should die happy.' This petition won the day. The Provost and Fellows of Oriel College gave permission, a plot of land and £100 besides.

On July 16th 1835 John Henry wrote jubilantly to Hurrell Froude: 'My chapel, (Littlemore) was begun yesterday and the first stone is to be solemnly laid next week. It is to be roofed in by the end of October. The two builders ran against each other, £663 to £665, the architect beforehand reckoning on £650, so I hope I have got it at about the right sum. This takes in everything of fitting up, except the bell.' Collecting was to continue throughout the year. John Henry approached his many friends, all the leading Tractarians made donations but the Littlemore villagers more than met their share. John Henry kept a ledger, writing down, even with the children, pennies given and the donor's name. A typical entry would be 'Received of Mr Greening, this 11th of November 1835, the sum of eight pounds, six shillings from persons in Littlemore towards the building of the new church.'

Mrs Newman was to lay the foundation stone. The honour was a fitting one for her contribution to the revival of a dying village was very great. Only two years before, when cholera swept through Oxfordshire, she showed her worth. One victim died in Littlemore, one in a neighbouring parish, so the risk of an epidemic was great. Mrs Newman wrote to her son from Rosehill 'Should the cholera increase, I wish you would have that cottage at Littlemore for headquarters for nurses to be on the spot, without mixing with uncontaminated families, and for a depot for medicines etc. I should think it a privilege, while health permits, for you to consider me head nurse. I have the whole in my head, should it be ordained that our vicinity is to suffer under the visitation. Pray take care of your own health. Your usefulness is before you, I trust for the comfort of many, for many years.'

In her pocket-book, at the end of the great day, Mrs Newman wrote 'July. Tuesday 21st A gratifying day. I laid the first stone of the church at Littlemore. The whole village there, The Hackers, Thompsons, Keble, Eden, Copeland. J. H. a nice address, Prayers, Creed and the old Hundreth Psalm.'

2 A CHURCH FOR LITTLEMORE

HOW SWIFTLY THE sands of time may shift. When Mrs Newman laid the foundation stone of the new church, benefactors rejoiced, the architect had his plans, materials were ready; even the workmen, we are told, arrived early that the building should be finished on time. John Henry had fifteen children ready for confirmation with their catechism answers pat. Yet, a year later, when the church was almost ready for consecration, the Newman family had vanished and their house, Rose Bank, was up for sale.

Jemima began it all when she said 'Yes' to John Mozley, who worked in his father's printing press at Derby and came down to Oxford in 1835 to visit his brothers James and Tom. On arrival, he first called at Oriel to find John Henry busy compiling a tract. Next, he went to Rose Bank to greet Mrs Newman and Jemima about whom he wrote in a letter 'Miss Jemima is, as you have heard, not handsome, but is certainly a very pleasing person. She is more like Mr Newman than her sister. At times there is, both in expression and tone of voice, a very strong resemblance.'

John later met Jemima at the Bodleian Library and they went together to a lecture on fossil fishes by a Dr Buckland, who made many small jokes 'not, perhaps, quite to be expected of an Oxford professor.' Next, Mrs Newman took Jemima to visit John's parents in Derby and the wedding was fixed for April 28th 1836. As the new church was not quite ready, John Henry performed the ceremony in Iffley church. Mrs Newman could not attend the marriage—she was slightly indisposed—but she was in excellent spirits for the reception at Rose Bank. The young couple drove off for their honeymoon at Richmond, Windsor and Cambridge; the parting with the Littlemore children was very painful 'tears and sobs were very long and not to be comforted'.

Three weeks later, while they were in Cambridge, they heard of Mrs Newman's collapse. Even John Henry at Oriel only just reached Rose Bank in time; he and Harriett were with Mrs Newman when she died. She was sixty three. They buried her in St Mary's, in a vault inside the chancel. Isaac Williams, the curate, who buried her had, later, to arouse John Henry, kneeling at the side, deep in prayer. Yet more than one witness noted that once the funeral was over, John Henry more than recovered his cheerfulness and calm. His memorial to his mother may be seen in Littlemore Church today.

Harriett was the last to leave Rose Bank. She was so lonely in the house. Jemima invited her to Derby and from there she wrote to John Henry for his blessing; Tom Mozley, John's brother and a Fellow of Oriel, had proposed to her. John Henry approved. He told Jemima that he thought the suggested date, Sept. 27th, too near to her mother's funeral but said nothing to Harriett herself. Indeed, he sent her £30 for her trousseau and asked Tom Mozley to take all the furniture and plate from Rose Bank. He wrote 'It would be the greatest comfort to be free from the charge of both, without breach of duty'. When the Church at Littlemore was consecrated, Newman was back in his rooms at Oriel. He wrote to Harriett who understood his loneliness 'God intends me to be lonely. He has so framed my mind that I am, in great measure, beyond the sympathies of other people and thrown upon Himself.'

Though John Henry loved his mother and mourned her sincerely, he returned to his rooms in Oriel, I suggest, with a deep sense of relief. His financial burdens had increased.

John Henry was now thirty five and had been helping to
support the family since he was twenty three. His brother
Frank, prickly and eccentric, had once rebuked him for
letting his mother live too well. A year before her death,
John Henry was even asking God for financial help. He
told his sister Jemima of his plight. Now, with his mother's
death, a scruple assailed him that God had answered his
prayer in this vigorous way. In times of mourning, many
are tempted to worry, when looking back.

A further menace had been looming up, still shapeless,
but one from which he could not escape. In the earlier
days, he had sent his mother all his sermons and she had
loved them and even sent him suggestions for other
sermons with appropriate texts. In more recent years, she
found his sermons far above her head. His sister Harriett
went further, wanted to speak to him about them, found
his new views too high for her. Mrs Newman was a simple,
practical soul with no theology, beyond a love of the Bible
and an ingrained dislike of Rome. She read the religious
papers with their mounting bitter attacks on her son as a
secret Romanist He, too, hated Rome but had drawn from
his study of the Fathers a vision of a pure, primitive
Catholicism, free of Roman corruptions; a vision which
she could not share.

Forty years later, looking back, John Henry drew up a
short statement which he called 'Apology for Myself.' In
it, he accepted the fact that they all had been wrong in
arranging for the family to live near together, for his other
work engrossed him, they did not see him so often and
took this as a sign that he did not care. 'There was always
the chance of their not liking those whom I liked and, in
matter of fact, they did not like some of my greatest
friends. And again, from the first, they did not like the
distinctive principles of the Oxford Movement and the

more it developed, the wider did their differences from me in respect to it grow ... They had a full right to their own views but I did not imitate them in patiently bearing what could not be helped.'

Littlemore church

Dedication

With so much shock and sorrow in the background, the consecration of the Chapel of St Mary, the Virgin and St Nicholas on September 22nd 1836 proved, surprisingly, a most joyous event. John Henry himself, in a letter next day, gave his impressions:

> The day was fine and, as you may suppose, the chapel full, Williams read and I preached. The East end is quite beautiful. We had a profusion of bright flowers, in bunches, all about the chapel. The Bishop was much pleased. There were a number of details which made it a most delightful day, and long, I hope, may it be remembered here. Two children were baptised afterwards.

Bishop Bagot of Oxford put his feelings on paper that very day. He wrote to John Henry 'I was so much pleased with your sermon today that I should feel much gratified and obliged if you would allow me to read it' and added, when returning it 'Many thanks for your sermon. I have read it with sincere delight.'

Bloxam Arrives

One other spectator, a complete stranger, would write to John Henry, about the consecration in 1886, fifty years to the day. John Rouse Bloxam, D.D. put his feelings this way:

> I do not forget that it is now fifty years since I had the privilege of making your acquaintance and, eventually, obtaining your friendship. In September 1836, I had just come into residence as Fellow of Magdalen College and was furnishing my rooms when, on the 20th, I, not by accident I think, walked up to Littlemore and seeing the chapel door open, entered. You were alone, placing the stone cross over the altar. Turning round and seeing a stranger, you asked me if I thought it threw sufficient shadow?
>
> On the 22nd, I was present at the consecration and I fancy that you and I are the only survivors of the adults who were there ... Then I wrote and offered my services as curate and you answered me civilly that Isaac Williams was appointed—but not long afterwards you invited me to dinner to meet Keble to my great delight and that was the commencement of the brightest era of my life.

Dr John Rouse Bloxam, D.D.

Always modest, Bloxam does not mention that he had
volunteered to serve as curate without pay. Nor did he
have reason to state that, soon afterwards, he became
curate of Littlemore, that he added five stained-glass
windows to the little church, two of which survive today.
Littlemore owes much to him. As curate he supervised the
building of the little school, adjoining the churchyard.
Today, the school is much larger but his two classrooms,
still in use, may easily be identified.

On June 27th 1879, old Cardinal Newman, so recently
honoured, crossed the Channel and rested in Brighton for
two nights. He was seventy-eight. This did not stop him

from taking the local train to Beeding to greet the Vicar, Dr John Rouse Bloxam, D.D.

Interior of Littlemore Church

'I am tempted to pitch my tent here'

The chapel of St Mary and St Nicholas was unpretentious, seating two hundred and consisting only of a nave. It gained some notice in the press and a picture in one journal, in praise of its simplicity of style. Later, it would be described as 'a very early example of simple Gothic Revival', a thought which would have made John Henry

smile. More important for him, his chapel gave Littlemore
a living centre and a possible link with former times. As
the site was cleared, human remains were uncovered to
the right and left of the building, suggesting an earlier
graveyard, possibly a church.

Visitors should note that the tower and chancel were
added to the building two years after John Henry had bid
Littlemore farewell. The stone altar and reredos were his
and caused some worry before the Dedication; some
friends thought that the bishop might judge it too Romanist. In fact, Dr Bagot was much impressed. Other
Newman relics in the church are Bloxam's two surviving
windows and the memorial to Mrs Newman in which the
chapel, then a building, may be discerned. Most moving
memory is the tribute to benefactors—among them nearly
all the great Tractarians and, typical of John Henry, with
the parishioners having pride of place.

John Henry now had a church but still no vicarage. He
went back to his rooms in Oriel and, in 1837, Bloxam, as
curate, had to find digs. A few yards down from the church
were a huddle of cottages round *The George*, an old coach-
ing inn. *The George* had stables in the rear, a forge, and
limited accommodation. Bloxam found lodgings with Mr
and Mrs Barnes. It is impossible to identify his apartment
but he had a ground floor room. From this base, Bloxam
supervised the building of the school, and beautified the
church with five stained-glass windows and a lectern; he
wanted to place two antique chairs in the sanctuary but
John Henry said no. Bloxam was an antiquarian and ritualist; and was to become one of the first clergymen in Oxford
to popularise and sport a stole. Bloxam was a patient man.
Because Littlemore was not yet an independent parish, it
now had not one but two earnest parsons striding up and
down Rose Hill. John Henry still went to visit his parish on

occasion while Bloxam, as a fellow of Magdalen, had work in college in mid-week.

John Henry was less than happy at Oriel. He mourned his mother, missed his sisters and the house off Rose Hill. After ten years, he was now a Senior in the Common Room; his contemporaries had married and moved to rural parishes. St Mary's drew bigger and bigger crowds for his Sunday sermons but he was older and they, much younger men. His influence was impressive, his reputation national. He was still enthusiastic; in 1837 he began his soirées every Monday evening with nine or ten invited to attend. Many would, later, recall these evenings, John Henry's skill, the wide variety of topics; one undergraduate wrote in a letter 'He talks to me of every sort of subject except what is called Tractarianism.'

After a faltering start, the Tracts had worked wonders and were all the rage. With success came sorrow, even bitterness. Much has been published about religious hostilities in Oxford, with Evangelicals, Peculiars, High and Dry, Tractarians at each other's theological throats. John Henry's novel *Loss and Gain* gives his opinion, looking back. No love was lost among the sectaries but they came together on one common issue, a universal hatred and distrust of Rome. What is more, John Henry joined the pack. He preached against Roman corruption and a friend noted down eleven violent expressions with some glee. Young Frederick Faber, a future Oratorian, attended an anti-Catholic lecture, and thought Mr Newman magnificent. John Henry himself composed a series of anti-Romanist tracts and even toyed with a display card, to inform customers in friendly shops. John Henry failed. An older and experienced critic read one of these tracts and told John Henry of his impressions, that the denunciations of Roman corruptions were admirable but failed to eliminate the craving 'she has much that we want.'

This, of course, is the truth. John Henry and the Tractarians did not want to be Romanist or Protestant. Over ten years of earnest study of the writings of the Primitive Fathers, they had discerned a faint outline of a Middle Way. John Henry, in the Tracts, liked to call this the *Via Media*, a Latin phrase. Tractarians were sincere. The Reformation recipe could no longer meet their aspirations; the first Apostles never taught Private Judgment, Faith Alone, the Bible Only, while *By Law Established* was less convincing now that parliament was filled with legislators of mixed and contradictory beliefs. On the other hand, Rome was regarded with hatred and suspicion; it had added Mariolatry, Indulgences and other obvious corruptions to the primitive purity of Apostolic faith.

The very few Roman Catholics in England favoured retirement and few Protestants contacted them. Bloxam was one and his visit to Lord Shrewsbury at Alton Towers cost him dearly; an informant told Newman that Bloxam had not only attended Mass but bowed his head, and Newman felt bound to report the matter to the Bishop. To see the Catholic Church in action, one had to cross the channel and this John Henry and a few friends had done. Dr Pusey, Hurrell Froude, Archdeacon Manning, sister Harriett and her husband, Tom Mozley, came home shocked, often disgusted but, also, curiously impressed.

Early in 1840, Bloxam resigned his curacy. He had been acutely embarrassed by the Alton Towers incident, and also his father was gravely ill. John Henry wrote to him 'What a loss I have in you, my dear B, I feel it most acutely … you have inspired a great reverence for religion and love of the Church and I see it in more ways than I can name.'

Yet Bloxam's departure from Littlemore was to have a profound effect on John Henry's career. Though remaining Vicar of St Mary's and preaching there, Sunday after Sunday, John Henry decided to leave his new curate, William Copeland, in St Mary's while he himself—for Lent 1840—would reside in Littlemore. He moved to Bloxam's lodging near *The George* with his dear friends Tom and Mary Barnes to look after him. Mrs Barnes went into action at once. John Henry had a bad cold and writes to Jemima 'Mrs Barnes comforts me by telling me that, if I take some precious mess (which now stands on my fender, till I go to bed) for three nights, I cannot tell the deal of good it will do me.'

John Henry was severe to himself during this Lent. He recited the breviary every day and this took several hours at the start. We find him sleeping on the floor now and then and curtailing his diet daily, with added severity during Holy Week. As he never spoke to others about these exercises and records the details only in private notebooks, let us leave things there. To form a fair judgment of his motives we need to read his *Church of the Fathers*, published for the first time in book form in that very year. His two chapters about St Antony, the hermit, supply a sane and thoughtful account of his aims and objects and the plan which explains all that was to happen at Littlemore.

Whatever his austerities in private, this first stay in Littlemore was to prove one of the happiest in John Henry's Oxford life. 'For myself', he wrote to Bloxam ' I am so drawn to this place, though I have been here but a week that it will be an effort to go back to St Mary's ... If it were not for those poor undergraduates who are, after all, not my charge and the Sunday Communions, I should be sorely tempted to pitch my tent here.' He told Jemima 'I am catechizing the children in Church on Sundays and prepare them for it through the week. I have morning prayers daily as well as afternoon'. Both Jemima and Bloxam must have smiled when he wrote 'I have rummaged out an old violin and strung it and on Mondays and Thursdays have begun to lead them with it, a party of between twenty and thirty, great and little, in the schoolroom.' He asked for Gregorian music but when he had some, he found the children hesitant 'it makes them smile' he writes 'though that may be at me.'

Littlemore church and school

That Lent, John Henry's catechism classes in Littlemore were known in Oxford. James Mozley wrote home 'Men have gone out of Oxford every Sunday to hear it. I thought it very striking, done with such spirit and the children so up to it.' Pages could be filled with John Henry's goings on with the children at Littlemore. He had trouble with the girls—the eldest ten—who had never been taught to wash. He found the teacher a 'dawdle and do-nothing' and suspected that she was drinking and admitted, finally, to Tom Mozley 'She does drink badly.' Let us leave John

Henry and his children on a higher note, penned to
Bloxam 'The children are vastly improved in singing and,
now that the organ is mute, their voices are so thrilling as
to make one sick with love.'

On March 28th 1840, Bloxam's father died. Though no
longer John Henry's curate, Bloxam, on his return to
Oxford, hurried up to Littlemore. As he, later, described
it, on reaching Barnes' cottage 'As I passed the window, I
saw him kneeling in prayer.' John Henry mentions
Bloxam's return in a letter to Jemima, thanking his two
sisters for a very precious gift. Rarely in a long life-time
did he express such spontaneous happiness:

Littlemore. April 18th 1840

> I have just ended the Lenten fast and Bloxam has
> come up and taken tea with me. Then we went to
> church and with much care arranged the altar cloth
> ... It looks beautiful. As to Mrs Barnes, she
> dreamed of it, from astonishment at its elaborate-
> ness; and Eliza B. and several others, who are
> workwomen, look at it with amazement ... Indeed
> we are all so happy that we are afraid at being too
> happy. We have got some roses, wallflowers and
> sweet-briar and the Chapel smells as if to remind
> one of the Holy Sepulchre. Really I have everything
> my own way and I quite dread some reverse,
> because I am so favoured.

Three days later he wrote to his dear friend Rogers
'Considering I have little or nothing to do at Oxford,
parochially, and a great deal to do at Littlemore, I naturally
feel a desire to reside at Littlemore rather than at Oxford.'

This is a Secret

John Henry returned to Oxford in May 1840 but he left his heart in Littlemore. This he revealed when he shared a secret with three of his most intimate friends. He divulged his plan first to Bloxam and asked his assistance: 'What would you say if I am thinking of wheedling Mr Laffer out of some land to build a monastery on? This is a secret. I am using your name as more influential than my own.' Bloxam, of course, was delighted and, also, very successful. Mr Laffer was a tough old farmer but Bloxam was a persuasive man.

Memorial plaque to Jemima Newman in Littlemore church

Writing to Frederic Rogers from Littlemore, John Henry did not mention a monastery but a hall. 'But, next, supposing I took theological pupils at Littlemore, might not my house be looked upon as a sort of Hall, depending on Oriel?' He added 'Supposing a feeling arose in favour of monastic establishments and my house at Littlemore was obliged to follow the fashion and conform to a rule of discipline, would it not be desirable that such institutions should flow from the Colleges of our two Universities? ... I do not wish this mentioned by Hope to anyone else.' It should be noted that the idea of theological students was not wholly Newman's; the experiment on a small scale had been tried by Newman and some others in St Aldate's.

To his brother-in-law, Tom Mozley, an amateur architect, John Henry is more precise 'We have bought nine acres and want to build a monastic house.' (John Henry uses a Greek word which is best rendered thus). 'Give me some hint about building. My notion is to build a bit and then stop, but to build it on a plan which will admit of being added to. Were I a draughtsman, I would hit off something good; as it is, take the following (with a plan).'

John Henry elaborates his plan:

1. The library admits of increase along one side and is to be lighted by upper windows only, the room being 16 to 18 ft high'.

2. The cells are to be, as required, being (say) 9–10 ft. high.

3. The oratory or chapel a matter altogether for future consideration

4. I want a cell to contain about three rooms; a sitting room, 12 by 9, a bedroom 6 by 6 a cold bathroom, 3 by 3.

Two weeks later, Tom Mozley received another bright idea. John Henry suggested having

> the cells upon a cloister as at Magdalen and the library too. I meant to have asked before, whether I could not get rid of chimneys and fireplaces by pipes of hot water or would this be a great expense? The saving of chimneys, grates, etc., would be great. I would have a fireplace only in the kitchen and refectory, I am thinking of planting, in the autumn, two acres with larch and fir with more tender trees, yet suited to the soil, such as hornbeam etc., etc.

On May 28th 1840, John Henry wrote to Jemima letting her know of his plans:

> What a beautiful spring this has been after the last four bad years. We have bought nine or ten acres of ground at Littlemore, the field between the Chapel and the Barnes', and, so be it, in due time, shall erect a monastic house upon it. This may lead ultimately to my resigning my fellowship; but these are visions as yet. The children are improving their singing; we hope to be able to chant the whole service with them.
>
> My library is in most apple-pie order. I suppose I shall soon make it over to the parties who hold these nine acres. The tracts are most flourishing.

The last we hear of the Monastery is in a letter to Jemima on November 15th. Bloxam and the Magdalen planter had helped him and the new trees were in. He writes 'We have finished our planting at Littlemore and it looks very nice. By the time I am an aged person, if ever I am so, it will make a show.'

A few months later, March 9th and 12th 1841, John Henry wrote to Harriett:

> I have got into what may prove a serious mess here.
> I have just published a Tract (No. 90) which I did
> not feel likely to attract attention. I fear I am clean
> dished. The Heads of Houses are at this very
> moment concocting a manifesto against me. Do
> not think I fear for my cause.

My Books are on the move

Early in 1842 John Henry left his rooms in Oriel College
and moved to Littlemore for good. After the publication
of Tract 90 and the uproar which greeted it, he took several
months to make up his mind. In this, he obeyed the
counsel which he gave to others, never to act in haste. As
he wrote to a friend in December 1841:

> In consequence, for two years past, my view of my
> duty and my prospective plans here have been very
> unsettled. I have had many schemes floating on my
> mind how to get out of a position which, of all
> others, is to me most odious—that of a teacher
> setting up for himself against authority, though, I
> suppose (if it may be said reverently) our Saviour
> bore this cross with others.

The controversy over Tract 90 should not be considered
here. It hardly concerns the villagers of Littlemore who
worried little about the Thirty-nine Articles and their
meaning in the reign of Queen Elizabeth I. Newman and
the Tractarians saw a contradiction between the Articles
and the Creed, between professing belief in the Catholic
and Apostolic Church and then interpreting the Articles
in a rigid, Protestant sense. Both sides of the debate may
be studied in innumerable books and pamphlets and, some
fifteen years later, his *Apologia,* drew from John Henry a
brilliant account of his case. Sufficient here to recall that
Tract 90 was never officially condemned, that John Henry

never regretted its publication, that he was astonished at
the sudden fury, for all the previous Tracts had hinted as
much and more.

Memorial plaque in Littlemore church

John Henry broke the news to Jemima on January 19th
1842. He had to be careful for both his sisters were devoted
to him and expressed alarm in their letters when reports
from Oxford were bad. He wrote to her now:

> You may think that I have no *intention* of leaving
> St Mary's by the fact of my having taken a *lease* of

the cottages at Littlemore and having laid out a large sum of money on them but it is quite certain that an Archbishop's letter, admitted by my own Bishop, might be of a nature to drive me away.

Jemima must have puzzled about these cottages. Not so very long before, John Henry had been busy planning a monastery and planting two acres of trees.

He wrote her again three weeks later when the final step had been taken and the library, which he had been building up since boyhood, was on the move. He explained the situation:

I am going up to Littlemore for good and my books are all in motion—part gone; the rest in a day or two. It makes me very downcast; it is such a nuisance taking steps ... Of Tract 90, 12,500 copies have been sold and a third edition is printed. An American clergyman, who was here lately, told me he saw it in every house.

Oriel College Hall and Chapel

Ten days later, he added further details:

> I am in Oxford only on Saturday evening and
> Sunday morning. My books are all up but not my
> bookcases. You may think it makes me somewhat
> downcast but I don't know how I frightened you.
> For some years, as is natural, I have felt that I am
> out of place at Oxford, as customs are. Everyone
> almost is my junior. And, then, added to this, is the
> hostility of the Heads, who are now taking meas-
> ures to keep the men from St Mary's. But I think I
> have made up my mind, unless something very
> much out of the way happens, to anticipate them
> by leaving off preaching at St Mary's. I shall tell no
> one. My being up here is an excuse and I can at any
> time begin again. But I think my preaching is a
> cause of irritation and, for what I know, any
> moment they may do something against me at St
> Mary's and I would rather anticipate this ... A year
> and a half ago (as Harriett knows) I wanted to retire
> from St Mary's, keeping Littlemore.

From Littlemore, John Henry continued as Vicar of St
Mary's preaching weekly in Oxford to undaunted crowds
of enthusiasts for another eighteen months. Though he
had changed over the years and the congregations altered,
his sober, deeply spiritual sermons struck the same note
and the same response from first to last

We should, however, visit the rooms in Oriel, first floor
near the Chapel, which he occupied for some fifteen years.
When he wrote to Jemima 'My books are on the move', she
was able to decode the message, for his library ranked with
Littlemore as the absorbing joy of his personal, private life.
His rooms in Oxford were jammed with books. Tom Mozley
gives us the setting 'when strangers were daily coming to
Oxford and making it their first business to see the abode of
the man who seemed to be moving the Church of England

to its foundations, they were surprised to find that he had simply an undergraduate's lodging.' J. W. Burgon adds to this, one sentence: 'Ill carpeted and indifferently furnished as well as encumbered with bookshelves in every part.' John Henry rarely gave away a book. As a small boy he read Tom Paine's *Rights of Man*, universally frowned on, but he clung to his copy and had it at Oriel, under lock and key, to be loaned to mature men.

John Henry's library is now in Birmingham, he carted it from place to place. Anyone who had the time would probably find on the shelves John Henry's copies of Scott, Thackeray, Jane Austen, Trollope, Gibbon, Butler, some of his favourites. In the library, now in Birmingham, are the works of the Primitive Fathers of the Church which John Henry asked Dr Pusey to buy for him in Germany 'huge fellows they are but very cheap—one folio costs a shilling.' St Athanasius was, ever, John Henry's favourite and the volume which they show in Birmingham once belonged to Bossuet.

In 1831, ten years before Tract 90, John Henry came home from a walk and found in his rooms, thirty six glorious folios of the Fathers, a gift from his students when his days as a tutor were done.

Let Bloxam, the most deserving, tell us about Newman's College rooms:

> You entered from a staircase by a door in the corner of the room. On your left were two windows looking into the quadrangle, opposite to them two windows, looking into Merton Lane; between the latter were engravings of St Christopher and the three different portraits of King Charles I in one print. On the other side of the door were bookcases filled with folio volumes of the Fathers. Opposite to these was the fireplace over which was a small portrait of his mother and a crucifix from which,

however, the figure had been removed. In the
centre of the room was a table covered with books
and papers. Newman's own chair was on one side
of the fireplace, near the table, with its back to the
Merton Lane windows.

Outside Oriel College

3 THE COLLEGE

NOT A FEW people confuse the College with the embryo monastery which John Henry was planning in 1840 when he stayed in Littlemore for Lent. Though he bought a field, planted trees, consulted Tom Mozley about central heating, the monastery was little more than a dream. John Henry was a determined man and would have brought his plan to fruition had not Tract 90 intervened.

The College was an improvisation to meet a crisis, only John Henry's motive stayed the same. In her classic biography, Miss Meriol Trevor sums up the situation well 'He had stopped talking about a monastery but this seemed a providential opportunity to begin living a life in accordance with some kind of rule.' He could not do this in Mrs Barnes' cottage. Down the road from the church, just hidden by the bend, was a row of stables, L-shaped, on the corner of the lane on the edge of the property he had bought. When in January 1842 he informed Jemima 'I have taken a lease of the cottages at Littlemore', the plan for the College was well advanced. We find him buying cheap furniture, fixing temporary lodgings and living at Littlemore in the summer of 1841.

The College was originally used as a stable by a Mr Costar who ran an Oxford-to-Cambridge coach. He had a barn, a stable or two and a few mean cottages, giving on to the yard. Coaches were being displaced by the railways and, though Littlemore had its station rather later, Costar's stables were in a sorry state. John Henry was first attracted by the barn which might hold his library while the cottages could be turned into cells.

Oxford Cambridge Coach

Jemima and Harriett had worked in Littlemore and knew the village well. Yet when Harriett later visited the College, she wrote to her sister 'John's new rooms are in a place neither you or I know. It looked like a wall. Now it has a dozen windows—one storey. Inside it is very pretty and neat—just my fancy. I do not wonder at John's present enthusiasm'.

John Henry spent much time in Littlemore during the winter of 1841. He was still preaching, still had his rooms in Oriel, but his interests were in Littlemore. He could not live with Mr Barnes, for his new curate, Mr Copeland, seems to have lodged there and, besides, John Henry wanted to be near the College to supervise the work. Just beyond the College, but across the road, there still stands a fine stone farmhouse behind a high wall. Recusant Catholics had lived there once. St George's, as it was called, was owned at the time by a Mr Giles, a farmer, who gladly gave the Vicar rooms. John Henry had a bedroom upstairs and a ground floor study; a story survives that John

Henry's name or initials were cut on a small diamond window which was later stolen, so they say.

John Henry spent the winter encouraging the workmen, especially Drunken Jim Blazy, who had to be supervised. In January 1842, when his library was in motion, the barn was ready with fitted bookshelves in place. John Henry carried so many books that one thumb was damaged and troubled him for years. In February he reported

> I have got all my books nearly in place and talk of insuring them; not, one would trust, that there is much danger of fire but I am somewhat given to fancy mischances and, when they are insured, I shall be dwelling on the chance of their being destroyed, as Dr Priestley's, by a mob shouting 'No Popery in 1780', in which case the insurance would not hold. The dwelling-rooms are still in a damp state awaiting for the March winds to blow through them.'

First Description of the College

The first description of John Henry's scheme is found in the letter of a young graduate of Exeter College to a friend. John Dobree Dalgairns had wind of John Henry's activities and wrote:

> His scheme about Littlemore goes on and I love to cherish a vision of one day being there with him, though I am quite aware that it is a mere vision. You would smile if you saw the embryo monastery. It is nothing else but a sort of angular farm-yard and offices with windows knocked into the granary wall, the stable being converted into a library. It is this shape:—

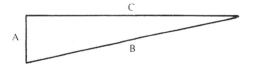

The two sides A and B being the library and
dwellings, C being the wall. There is a sort of green
veranda running along B and numerous shrubs are
planted in the middle. There you have the whole
monastery of The Cottages, for such is the techni-
cal term. Bloxam also calls it the Union Workhouse; it certainly does look vastly like its name.
However, there have been more unpromising
establishments to start with and Newman's library
beats most monkeries to sticks. I believe it will be
ready next Lent.

The Press get it wrong

Just a week before John Henry moved into the College, he
received a very different description of his project from an
eminent friend. Dr Bagot, Bishop of Oxford, had always
tried to be fair to Newman. At the dedication of the
Chapel, he had expressed delight and borrowed John
Henry's sermon. Later, against much pressure, he never
condemned Tract 90, though he cannot be said to have
approved of it. He now wrote:

> So many of the charges against yourself and your
> friends which I have seen in public journals have
> been, within my own knowledge, false and calum-
> nious that I am not apt to pay much attention to
> what is asserted in respect to you in the newspa-
> pers. In a newspaper, however, of April 9th, there
> appears a paragraph in which is asserted as a
> matter of notoriety that a so-called Anglo-Catholic
> monastery is in process of erection in Littlemore
> and that the cells of dormitories, the chapel, the
> refectory, the cloisters, all may be seen advancing
> to perfection under the eyes of a parish priest of
> the Diocese of Oxford.

John Henry answered his bishop courteously. He assured His Lordship 'No monastery is in process of erection, there is no chapel, no refectory, hardly a dining-room or parlour, the cloisters are my shed, connecting the cottages.' John Henry goes on to explain his purpose, calling his building a parsonage-house, pointing out that the population in Littlemore is at least equal to that of St Mary's and that he plans to live in Littlemore until the prevailing excitement dies down.

> With a view to personal improvement, I was led more seriously to a design which has long been on my mind. For many years, at least thirteen, I have wished to give myself a life of greater regularity than I have hitherto led.

This explanation produces a further problem, what name to give to John Henry's Parsonage-house. Today, it is officially called The College, never in Newman's time. Contemporary Oxford knew it as The Monastery. After John Henry's departure, it is called, in an early directory, The Priory. To many old villagers, it is the Reading Room. Yet one old man with a splendid memory had it from his parents that when they were young the present College passed as 'Mr Newman's cottages.'

The First Arrivals

The College opened its door—it had only one—on April 19th 1842. John Henry, the Vicar, alone entered and made for rooms at the end of the cloister or shed. As far as we know, he kept to those rooms for the next four years. In a letter he described the situation 'I have just come here and must set things going and that requires close residence for a while. At this very moment, I am literally *solus,* without servants or anything else but I suppose we shall accumulate in time.'

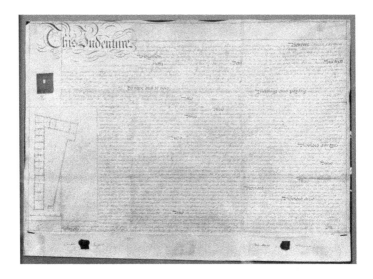

The College Lease

He had few plans. He knew of one or two who would probably join him but he was accurate in telling the bishop that he was building a parsonage-house. The College was first and foremost his vicarage from which he served the Chapel and his people every day. Many casual visitors came and went across four years. He was not exaggerating to the bishop when he saw his College as a place for study and private personal prayer. Throughout the four years John Henry kept his own programme, not unrelated to his book *The Church of the Fathers* and the disciplines practised there. Yet he still had in mind the suggestion he had made to Rogers of welcoming students to share his life and library. He knew the need. Many young graduates and curates, ardent Tractarians or Anglo-Catholics, were now being harassed in college, even refused ordination by various bishops if they showed Tractarian tendencies.

John Dobree Dalgairns, as we might have guessed, was the first to arrive. A lively young graduate of twenty four, Dalgairns, a native of Guernsey and bi-lingual, had troubles not only in college but from his parents at home. He had Roman leanings and the College at Littlemore being firmly Anglo-Catholic, afforded a convenient check.

Dalgairns, a prolific letter-writer, provides our first eyewitness account.

> As to the Union Workhouse, it really and truly as yet is to be nothing more than a place where men who have no fellowships may come to read under Newman's inspection and with his library, which is an excellent one. As, however, there cannot be persons enough living here to fill the rooms, any country parson who likes to retire there for a session will be welcome. I have said *As Yet*, because I am sure (though there are very few persons to whom I would say so) that Newman means, if possible, to establish some sort of rule in time, whether strict or not he does not know but will be guided by circumstances. While I am on the subject, I may as well say that you be under no apprehension as to Newman going over to Rome.

Within a month from opening the College, John Henry's sister Harriett arrived. She brought with her Tom Mozley, her husband, and their little daughter Grace. Harriett was delighted for everyone called Grace 'You little darling' or 'Little pet'. Harriett's description is interesting for it supplies a female touch:

> There are 4 or 5 sets of rooms—sitting and bedroom—all on the ground floor,—the door opening onto a verandah which runs all along, a length of the diagonal of the Oriel Quad. The kitchen is in the middle—a pretty little garden before the verandah. At right angles is the library, a large pretty

room with a nice roof, the sides covered with books. Inside, another small bookroom and, above, a spare bedroom.

Mr Dalgairns is his companion—he was reading in the library, a modest looking, blushing youth—all the men again talking of his beauty and fine eyes. I thought him nothing but a boy with no harm about him and particularly clean looking. The new windows were putting up, very old and handsome looking.

Tom, Harriett and Grace Mozley

No official College booklog seems to have survived. But for Dr Bloxam's industry, our knowledge would have been very thin. A cautious man, Dr Bloxam never seems to have slept in the College though he visited Littlemore from time to time. With no scrap of evidence, one has the impression

that some old friends were slightly afraid. If so, Bloxam
made full amends. His love for John Henry was such that
he filled three vast scrapbooks, now in Magdalen College,
crammed with cuttings, cartoons, memories of John
Henry's life. Forty years later, he would be pestering
former inmates—Stanton, Bowles, St John, Christie—for
details of College life.

Thanks to Bloxam, we know that two boys, Woodma-
son and Welch, came to the College daily for lessons, that
Dalgairns caught a cold and coughed so much that they
moved him to the room upstairs. John Henry sat in the
smaller bookroom when it was his turn to answer the front
door bell. Bloxam also preserves Charles Marriott's
comment after a stay in 1842:

> I am spending a day or two with Newman in his
> parsonage at Littlemore where he leads almost a
> monastic life, giving the whole morning to study
> and devotion. The quiet that reigns here is new to
> me and very favourable to reflection, though I
> doubt whether I am equal to such a life myself.

Two other earnest young Tractarians came to the College
and left us detailed accounts. Mark Pattison, later Rector
of Lincoln College, Oxford, kept a diary during his stay of
some ten days in October 1843. He describes walks to
Garsington and Sandford, his conversations with John
Henry, his health, his efforts at prayer, the Eucharist at
Littlemore Church on Sunday—there were 37 communi-
cants. J. A. Froude, the future historian, came to the library
to work. Commenting on John Henry's *Apologia,* written
twenty later, Froude writes 'The *Apologia,* is the most
beautiful of autobiographies but it tells us only how the
writer appeared to himself. We, who were his contemporaries can alone say how he appeared to us in the old days.'

Pattison and Froude are valuable witnesses. As under-graduates, they fell under Newman's spell and wrote glow-ingly about him but later both fell away. Froude in his years of unbelief, made John Henry a sinister figure in his novel *The Nemesis of Faith*, where Pattison, looking back, saw his escape from Tractarianism and John Henry as a relief. Yet in 1884, Cardinal Newman, aged 83, made the journey from Birmingham to Oxford for a most moving farewell to Mark Pattison who was dying and when the old Cardinal preached in London, J. A. Froude applied for a ticket of admission, writing 'if I could but hear that voice again.'

Lockhart

John Dobree Dalgairns was the first young graduate in residence, William Lockhart came in the summer of 1842. A relative of Sir Walter Scott, John Henry accepted him at the request of the Lockhart family who feared he might go over to Rome. William was twenty two and when accepted by John Henry, had promised him to remain for three years. Lockhart had been deeply moved by John Henry's sermons and for the first time in his life had become aware of personal sin. He had read Dr Pusey's tracts on Baptism which touched on the forgiveness of post-baptismal sin. No-one in Oxford seemed to know much about the Sacrament of Penance but he found some information from a fellow Scot, who had obtained a Papist book from a Catholic priest. This book, *The End of Controversy*, by old Bishop Milner, pointed out that Protestants, too, should believe in Confession for the sacrament is mentioned in the Prayerbook, in the rite of Ordination and the visitation of the sick.

Lockhart goes on from there

It was difficult to try Confession in the Anglican Church. However, I made the attempt as at least a moral discipline. Archdeacon Manning, whom I knew, was in Oxford for it was his turn to preach the University sermon. I went to confession to him in Merton Chapel, his own college. It was a relief to me for a time. He also gave me excellent advice and, I think, counselled me to put myself under Newman and to try to remain and take Orders in the Anglican Church. I tried to do so. I was admitted by Newman's great kindness as one of his first companions at Littlemore. I remained with him for about a year. The life was something like what we read of in *The Lives of the Fathers of the Desert*, of prayer, fasting, study. We rose at midnight to recite the Nocturnal office of the Roman breviary. I remember direct invocation of the saints was omitted and, instead, we asked God that the saint of the day might pray for us. I think we passed an hour in private prayer, and for the first time I learned what meditation meant. We fasted every day till twelve and in Lent and Advent until five. There was some mitigation on Sundays and the greater festivals. We went to Communion in the village church and to services every day. We went to confession every week.

At the humble start of the College, the inmates lived minute by minute with no immediate goal before them beyond study, fasting and prayer. It never dawned on them that their efforts might one day be important, that notes should be taken and kept. William Lockhart's account, here given, was written nearly fifty years later, at the time of John Henry's death. He and other witnesses vary as to details. We may not assert on his evidence that midnight office was sung or recited every night for four years; on his own admission, he stayed with John Henry only for one.

Drawing of the College

The College had been a mystery from the very beginning; Oxford called it the *Monastery* in a pejorative sense.
Monasteries had been swept away at the Reformation and
if a few communities had sought refuge in their native land
during the French Revolution, these were ignored by the
Protestant Establishment. Celibacy was no virtue, the
Roman liturgy a curruption, monasticism an alien cult to
be abhorred. Small wonder that a few undergraduates were
caught snooping round the buildings and a don or two
decided to exercise their horses near Littlemore. Inside
the College, Dalgairns added a P.S. to a letter 'Address all
letters to the Parsonage, Littlemore, if you would not have
the place set fire to.'

John Henry knew next to nothing about modern
monastic practice and discipline. Once years before, an
article by him defending Monachism had been criticised
and he had answered 'I can but throw myself upon the
General Church and avow, as I do, that if anyone will show
me any opinion of mine which the Primitive Church
condemns, I will renounce it; any which it did not insist
on, I will not insist on.' Arrangements at Littlemore
followed this rule of thumb. Apart from a rough time-table
for meals, each man was free. When Ambrose St John

joined the group, he expected that John Henry would plan his future but the reply came back 'It is no good attempting to offer advice when, perhaps I might raise difficulties instead of removing them. It seems to be quite a case in which you, as far as maybe, make up your mind for yourself. Come to Littlemore by all means. We shall rejoice in your company and, if quiet and retirement are able, as they very likely will be, to reconcile you to things as they are, you shall have your fill of them.'

Everything ran smoothly for a year. Then came a time when applicants were too many. John Henry wrote 'March 7, 1843. All our beds have been full for months and I think we must cut our sets of rooms in two to admit more inmates.' He himself did his house-work with the rest. He took his turn at the door, read aloud at some meals, played his violin of an evening, kept faithfully to the time-table but once overslept. He served at table to the bewilderment of little Emily Bowles, who had come to see her brother; she was tongue-tied when the great Mr Newman asked her 'Will you have some cold chicken?'

Lockhart puts it this way 'Newman would never let us treat him as superior but placed himself on a level with the youngest of us. I remember that he insisted on our never calling him Mr Newman, according to the custom at Oxford when addressing Fellows or Tutors of Colleges. He would have us call him simply Newman. I do not think we ever ventured on this, though we dropped the Mr and addressed him without a name.'

Lockhart leaves

It fell to William Lockhart to induce the final crisis which, sooner or later, had to be faced. On coming to Littlemore, he had promised to stay at the College for three years. We know his position for he later put it in writing 'We had a

sincere desire to remain in the Church of England if we
could be satisfied in so doing that we were members of the
world-wide, visible, communion of Christianity which was
of Apostolic origin.' This statement would have been
accepted by all Lockhart's fellow aspirants at the College
and by John Henry himself.

For Lockhart, the sacrament of penance was of peculiar
importance, as has been seen. His account goes on 'Once,
after confession, I said to Newman "Are you sure you have
the power of giving absolution?" He paused then said, in
a tone of deep distress, "Why will you ask me? Ask Pusey."
This was, I think, in the spring of 1843. It was the first
indication I had received that Newman had begun seri-
ously to doubt his position in the Anglican Church. I see
from his *Apologia* that his doubts as to whether the
Church of Rome was not altogether in the right and the
Church of England wholly in the wrong had taken root in
his mind about this time. I had promised him, soon after
going to Littlemore, that I would stay three years. He made
it a condition. I gave the promise but found it impossible
to keep. With great grief, I left my dear master and made
my submission to the Catholic Church.'

Last Oxford Sermon

John Henry Newman went to London on September 18th
1843 and resigned his living at St Mary's before a notary.
William Lockhart's flight was given as the reason though
John Henry went rather further and in a sad letter to Harriett
'I am not so zealous a defender of the established and
existing system of religion as I ought to be for such a post.'

John Henry preached his last sermon at St Mary's on
September 24th. Did the congregation know as he left the
pulpit that his voice would never more be heard? The
Provost of Worcester College was later embarrassed when

a student, on parting, said to him 'especially, Mr Provost, I am grateful to you for not having altered the dinner hour on Sundays so that my friends and I enjoyed to the last the benefit of hearing Mr Newman's sermons at St Mary's.'

Newman as a preacher

The Parting of Friends

At 11.00 a.m. on September 25th the chapel at Littlemore was crowded and there were chairs in the churchyard as well. Bloxam was there and, in his scrapbooks, saved every detail; the flowers round Mrs Newman's plaque, the children in their new dresses, a last gift from their Vicar, the officiating clergy, Dr Pusey, Mr Copeland, Mr Bowles.

140 people received Communion that day. Many were in tears when John Henry preached his 604th Anglican sermon, ending 'My friends, if you should be acquainted with anyone who, by his teaching or by his writings or by his sympathy has helped you or has seemed to understand you or feel with you, my friends remember such a one and pray for him.'

After the sermon, John Henry descended, took off his hood and left it hanging on a rail and 'it was felt by those present that this was a mark that he had ceased to be a teacher in the Church of England.

The Temporary Oratory

In a narrative restricted to Newman and Littlemore, outside activities would be out of place. Thus, the wrangles in Oxford must be passed over though the calling of Convocation was intended as a direct attack on Newman himself. C. P. Eden became the new Vicar of St Mary's, with William Copeland, a dear friend of John Henry's, as his curate, still living in Littlemore with Mrs Barnes. John Henry no longer officiated in the church but Copeland used to come to the College for prayers.

John Henry's retirement caused confusion among the undergraduates. A contemporary wrote 'No-one asked about it in public but everyone rushed to and fro to ask in private and recalled the last time Newman had been seen walking in the streets, how he had looked and what he had said? Twenty years later, Principal Shairp 'compared the scene in St Mary's, next Sunday, to the silence in a cathedral, when a great bell, tolling solemnly overhead, has suddenly gone still.' One scholar, hearing the rumours about resignation, lingered in the porch of St Mary's until the sermon had begun. Hearing Charles Marriott's voice, he braced himself, thought 'he is not too bad' and marched in.

Littlemore, three miles away, knew nothing of all this. For the villagers their Vicar was still at home, walking the streets, calling regularly on poor Elizabeth Lenthall who was dying of cancer, attending chapel services with others from the College every day. Three years later when her brother was leaving Littlemore as a Catholic, Jemima, on a last visit, found the villagers had no idea why he was going away.

Inside the College, applicants came and went as before. John Henry dined at Oriel once or twice, visited London to see a dear friend, Bowden, who was sick. Books were one of his worries, he writes in 1843 'Our library has been growing so much that I do not know how we will manage for room.' The obvious solution, to stop buying, did not occur to him.

As study was part of Newman's plan, the library had a part to play. As Lockhart put it 'It was his wish to give us some direct object for study, partly to keep us quiet, in his splendid library in which were all the finest editions of the Greek and Latin Fathers and the Schoolmen and all the best works on Scripture and Theology, general literature, prose and poetry and a complete set of the Bollandist *Acta Sanctorum,* so far as they had been then printed. He had a project of bringing out *Lives of the English Saints* and a translation of Fleury's *Ecclesiastical History.* I was set to work on the history of the Arian period with a view to undertaking the translation of a volume.' J. A. Froude, Mark Pattison, Dalgairns and Bowden were among those who tackled this work, which had been commenced three years earlier, at Newman's 'house for young writers' in St Aldate's.

The Oratory

With study went prayer in John Henry's programme and the last significant alteration to the College buildings links

up with this. All other residents had a sitting-room and
bedroom where John Henry had the two in one. He seems
to have favoured this arrangement earlier in his life. He thus
had one poor little room to spare which Dalgairns first
mentions in 1842. Dalgairns writes 'We do not go to chapel
(i.e. The Littlemore Chapel) for the breviary or English
morning services but say them in a most unchapel-like
room; we are only embryo monks and, therefore, it would
be humbug to get grand oratories.' John Henry took the
matter up with Bloxam in 1843—

> My dear Bloxam,
>
> My questions are these. We are fitting up a room
> for a temporary Oratory. Accordingly, we mean to
> have it hung round with curtains, as a mode of
> making it decent, yet without expending anything
> on the room itself—for the curtains will take down
> and move (as the Tabernacle). There is a window
> in (what must be) the East end, but so small and
> low that we think it better to cover it with curtains
> and have candles through the day. The Walls of
> the room are at present in part bare brick, yellow-
> washed. The dimensions are 16 ft. 2 ins. by 13 ft. 6
> inches and 9 ft. 2 ins. High. Now the question is
> what had we best do? If we have curtains, of what
> colour? May we have a quasi-altar?

Bloxam seems to have chosen red. The window is still
boarded up to prevent people looking in from the lane. A
shelf carries a crucifix and two candles. In John Henry's
day, candelabra in the centre allowed the community to
read their breviaries.

The College community went to Littlemore Church for
the Anglican daily service; they used the Oratory for the
Little Hours and, perhaps, for Vespers and Compline at
night. One or two Tractarians in the neigbourhood and

William Copeland joined them from time to time. From one of these we learn that the psalms were recited in Latin, using the Oxford pronunciation and the antiphons to Our Lady were left out. John Henry set much store by this. As he wrote to the future Father Faber 'I have a great repugnance in mixing religions or worships together. It is like sewing a field with mingled seed. I do not like decanting Rome into England.'

In 1843 in this small oratory, without windows, John Henry and some six companions made their first retreat. It was Holy Week. They knew nothing about the Spiritual Exercises of St Ignatius or of the normal retreat procedures and few, if any, of them had met a Catholic priest. For conferences, they used a booklet on the Spiritual Exercises composed by an unusual Jesuit, Fr Marmeduke Stone. They agreed to meet three times a day, at 4.30 a.m., 1.30 p.m. and 8.30 p.m. John Henry made many personal notes. Where St Ignatius suggests a short list of trials which the retreatant would try to face with Divine assistance, John Henry put down (1) having to make a General Confession to some one in our Church; I have not full faith that our Church has the power of Absolution, (2) having to join the Church of Rome, (3) having to give up my library.

1844–45

All was industry and bustle in the College to the very end. People came and went. When Lockhart moved out, Ambrose St John took his rooms at the top of the shed. Ambrose came for a visit but returned to be with John Henry for life. Frederick Bowles came in 1842 and stayed, Richard Stanton arrived more than two years later, John Walker turned up as late as September 1845. The last mentioned loved the piano and, hoping this was right in Advent, John Henry acquired one. Francis Knox appeared suddenly and had to be lodged, for the moment, in Dalgairns' room. Dalgairns himself well expressed the spirit of the College 'Newman declares his object is not to teach people austerities but only living in a plain, frugal way so as to get out of the gentleman-Parson line.' This is really the whole mystery of our pseudo-monastery. It is intended to be a place where a man may be silent and pray and read, and, if he will, be more austere than he can in the world.'

As for austerities, they were lucky to have Albany Christie with them, a medico from King's College Hospital, who spent his vacations at Littlemore. An Oriel graduate, Christie was refused ordination for Tractarian views, so trained as a doctor and obtained a Catholic pastoral letter to curb fasting extremes during Lent. He also helped in the village and the story survives that, when the Vicar asked a mother about her baby, she replied 'Please Sir, Mr Christie gave it a powder yesterday and this morning it died.'

The Development of Doctrine

Our story which began with a young Vicar, aged twenty-seven, inspecting his sprawling, rural parish, ends with the same Vicar, now forty-four, standing at his writing desk in his poverty-stricken room. Later, he would say why—he wrote 'I determined to write an essay on Doctrinal Development; and if, at the end, my convictions in favour of the Roman Church are not weaker, to make my mind up and seek admission to her fold. I acted upon this resolution in the beginning of 1845 and worked at my essay steadily into the Autumn.' John Henry's mind worked in this deliberate way.

Because no information came from Littlemore, rumours thrived. Nosey Parkers of all denominations cried in unison 'Why does he wait?' His enemies put it about

that he had fled abroad—good riddance to bad rubbish—
that he had always been a Papist, disguised as a vicar to
ensnare the young. Older Tractarian friends, who had
always loved him, could only suggest he was out of his
mind. Archdeacon Manning and Mr William Gladstone
bewailed together 'The Newman of 1843 is not the
Newman of 1842; nor is he of '42 the same with him in
1841.' The Roman Catholics were as bad. A scout was sent
to Littlemore for lunch. As the story goes, he returned
jubilant to Oscott in the evening; John Henry was wearing
grey trousers so the end was near.

John Henry knew nothing of all this. He was his kindly
self to those at the College but thinner and more haggard
as becomes an inspired writer absorbed by his infant book.
Only Dalgairns of those in the College thought that
Newman was disturbed in mind.

An Essay on the Development of Christian Doctrine is
in no sense charismatic, in every sense unique. Only the
author could have produced it, the one who was reared as
a devout Calvinist, who came to appreciate the validity of
Tradition and devoted some twenty years to the study of
the Fathers to discover the spirit of the Apostolic Church.
Newman's Essay is unique for he had no outside assistance.
He could not consult his Tractarian friends for their
development had finished. As for Roman Catholics, he had
rarely met a Catholic priest. Alone in his cold room, day
after day, standing at his writing desk, he worked through
century after century, starting with the development of
ideas, distinguishing between valid growth and the con-
trary corruptions, so many of which he had charged
against the Church of Rome. Papal Supremacy, Purgatory,
Mariolatry, the cult of saints, are tested in turn. Beyond
each historical research lies the greater concept of the
Development of Doctrine as a whole. In so factual a book,

critics might challenge this point or that point but John Henry's sense of the Development of Doctrine is now unwittingly accepted throughout the Christian world.

The preface was written last. John Henry wrote:

> Since the above was written, the Author has joined the Catholic Church. It was his intention and wish to have carried his Volume through the Press before deciding finally on this step. But when he had got some way in the printing, he recognised in himself a conviction of the truth of the conclusion to which the discussion leads, so clear as to supercede further deliberation. Shortly afterwards circumstances gave him the opportunity of acting upon it and he felt that he had no warrant for refusing to do so.

This preface ends '*Littlemore, October 6, 1845.*' and thus the name of a very small Oxfordshire village is now known to thoughtful people around the world.

The End of the College

The College ended as quickly and quietly as it began. Out of the blue, Dalgairns wrote to a friend 'the end may be nearer than we fancy', while Frederick Oakeley, looking back, recalls 'In the autumn of 1844, symptoms of what is familiarly called a break-up began to manifest themselves.' Oakeley saw these symptoms in Oxford, not in Littlemore. He was an older man, one year younger than John Henry. His public defence of Tract 90 cost him his post in London at the Chapel in Margaret Street. Oakeley saw the condemnation of W. G. Ward by Convocation as the signal which sent many young Tractarians off to Rome. W. G. Ward himself promptly married; he and his young wife were received into the Catholic Church in London and retired to a house near Littlemore, somewhere on Rose

Hill. In September 1845, Oakeley came to live with them. Both Ward and Oakeley came to the College for prayers and John Henry, after his conversion, went round to call on them.

Within the College reactions were surprisingly quick. Nothing had been planned yet all acted in unison. As John Henry put it 'One friend going, pulls others after him by words of love.' John Henry, toiling on his book, made no effort to hold others back. Ambrose St John had long made his desires clear. Dalgairns was expecting a visit from his parents and thought the meeting would be less painful if he had taken the final step. When all had gone John Henry wrote in a letter 'When they wept, it was as if I was losing my bowels.'

Ambrose St John made for Prior Park, near Bath. Dalgairns chose Aston Hall, Staffordshire where Dominic Barberi lived. Stanton, who was in Chorley, planned to go to Stonyhurst.

Albany Christie, wrote from London that unless John Henry forbade him, he would go to St George's, Southwark, on a certain date. Bowles presumably went home to neighbouring Abingdon.

4 THE FINAL STEP

JOHN HENRY WAS alone for part of a week. As he wrote in the Preface to his Essay, his mind was made up. His plan was to see the book through the Press and then, near Christmas, to seek admission into the Church. He would have gone with Oakeley to the poor little Catholic Chapel in St Clement's of which he later wrote to Jemima 'nor is it a slight trial, as you may suppose, except as faith overcomes it, to go to what to outward appearance is a meeting house.' This he was spared. Dalgairns moved fast. He left the College for Aston on September 27th, was received into the Church two days later and was back in Littlemore just before midnight on October 1st. He needed John Henry's permission. Fr Dominic Barberi had to visit the Passionist headquarters in Belgium and Dalgairns had asked him to stop at Littlemore on the way. John Henry was delighted and surprised Dalgairns by adding that he would be received then.

John Henry's Reception

Many accounts, friendly and unfriendly, have dramatised John Henry's final step. The Geoffrey Faber version sees the poor man, after his first confession, in a state of near collapse. We read 'St John and another disciple took him by the arms and helped him, stumbling and half-fainting to his bed.' Dalgairns, too, makes us all jumpy with his 'Will he—Won't he?' approach. Oakeley, the realist, stresses the atrocious weather, Dominic Barberi soaked to the skin, while the wind was strong enough to make the bell above the door of Newman's chapel toll.

For any would be convert, reception is a strain. To one as affectionate and reserved as John Henry, the decision was painful, but few converts in history better knew his own mind. In the week before Dominic came, John Henry resigned his Oriel Fellowship, managed to call back Bowles and Stanton to share the occasion with him and then wrote some thirty letters to the friends of a life-time, all the letters to be posted after the final step.

Letters to Mrs Bowden, Oct 8th, 1845

As our story moves towards the end, it may be better to let John Henry speak for himself. We may judge his attitude, his mind, his need for an external call, his gratitude towards the little Italian padre who was at that very moment, wet to the skin, on the outside of the Oxford coach. Dalgairns would meet him at *The Angel* and get him to Littlemore at 10.30 p.m.

The Angel Inn

My dear Mrs Bowden,

I am this night expecting Father Dominic, the Passionist, in his way from Aston in Staffordshire to Belgium, where he goes to attend the Chapter of his Order, and he, please God, will admit me tomorrow or Friday into what I believe to be the one true Fold of Christ. Two more of our party, Bowles and Stanton, are to be received with me. Christie, if you know him by name, who has been here all the Vacation, is to go, as today, to a Priest in London. These coincident movements were through sympathy more than anything else.

For myself, I found my work almost finished and the printing going on slow, and some friends objected both to Christmas and to Advent, as times when they would rather not be unsettled, so I determined to act at once. And since I had all along been obliged to act from my own sense of right, I was not sorry that an external call, as it might seem, should come, and cut short my time and remind me of the sudden summons of St Matthew or St Peter, and of the awful suddenness of the Judgment. So when Dalgairns, whom he admitted, asked Father Dominic here for a night on his way, I determined to avail myself of his coming. He does not yet know of my intention.

I have seen the Padre once, on St John Baptist' Day last year, when I showed him the chapel here. He was a poor boy, who (I believe) kept sheep near Rome and from his youth his thoughts have been most singularly and distinctly turned to the conversion of England. He is a shrewd, clever man, but as unaffected and simple as a child and most singularly kind in his thoughts of religious persons of our communion. I wish all persons were as charitable as I know him to be. After waiting nearly thirty years, suddenly his Superiors sent him to England without any act of his own. However, he has not laboured in conversions, but confined himself to missions and retreats among his own people. I believe him to be a very holy man.

I have so many letters to write that I must break off. I shall not send this until it is all over.

With most affectionate thoughts of all of you, I am my dear Mrs Bowden,

Most Sincerely Yours,

John H. Newman.

Bronze relief by Faith Tolkien of Dominic Barberi receiving Newman, which is in the Catholic parish church of Littlemore

Those visiting the College today, will find few traces of Dominic Barberi's visit. He arrived on Wednesday evening late and left on Saturday after Mass. Which room he occupied is not known for certain but he was in the library drying his clothes by the stove when John Henry entered and knelt down. John Henry started his General Confession that evening and completed it next day. Far from being carried to bed, John Henry seems to have written more letters that evening and was at his desk writing to Jemima at 5.30 a.m., on the following day. He, with Stanton and Bowles, were received into the Church next evening and made their first Communion on the following day. The temporary oratory had to be changed for the occasion for there was no altar. John Henry's reading desk was brought in from his room next door and is in the Chapel now.

When the College closed, John Henry took the reading desk with him to Oscott and wrote to Henry Wilberforce 'I have brought your little reading desk; I had not the heart to leave it behind. It formed part of the altar on which Fr Dominic offered Mass and from which I received my first Communion.' Oakeley adds two other significant details. While Father Dominic was in the College, he—Oakeley— could only guess that something unusual was happening for the College was closed. On the day Fr Dominic left for Belgium, the oratory was once more open for evening prayers. There were two changes. The Oxford pronunci- ation of Latin gave way to the Italian and the antiphon to Our Lady was sung for the first time.

John Henry saw to it that he spent his last night at Littlemore alone. He wrote on Feb. 20th 1846 'We are now clear and I have a day of peace, I have had a very trying leave-taking with Mrs Barnes, Mrs Palmer and Mrs Tombs. To leave the children in the school was enough to make one cry, if one were not so hard. It would have been a great relief to be able.' His last letter from Littlemore, Feb. 21st ends 'Another comfort amid the pain of quitting this place is the pleasant memory which attaches to it. In spite of my having been in such doubt and suspense, it has been the happiest time of my life, because so quiet. Perhaps, I shall never have such quiet again ... I must leave off, though unwillingly, for time gets on and I must once more go over the poor house before the fly comes.'

The School

Epilogue

The Rev. C. C. L. Buckwell, Vicar of Littlemore, passed on a story which most fittingly ends this little book. The story is fully authenticated and dated 1868.

> I was passing by the Church at Littlemore when I observed a man very poorly dressed leaning over the lych gate crying. He was to all appearances in great trouble. He was dressed in an old grey coat with the collar turned up and his hat pulled down over his face as if he wished to hide his face. As he turned towards me, I thought it was a face I had seen before. The thought instantly flashed through my mind it was Dr Newman. I have never seen him,

but I remember Mr Crawley had got a photo of Dr Newman. I went and told Mr Crawley I thought Dr Newman was in the village but he said I must be mistaken, it could not be. I asked him to let me see the photo, which he did. I then told him I felt sure it was. Mr Crawley wished me to have another look at him. I went and met him in the churchyard. He was walking with Mr St John...

John Henry wrote to Bloxam in 1877 'I was never in Oxford since I left in February 1846. I went to Littlemore with Father Ambrose St John on June 16th, 1868. I saw many of my old parishioners, the Crawleys and the incumbent. Of course when I saw my mother's monument, I could but cry.'

Bust of Newman in the garden at Littlemore

5 THE COLLEGE TODAY

Part I

THE STORY OF Newman at Littlemore must surely end with the College, the last visible reminder of John Henry's stay. When Bloxam dubbed it 'the Union Workhouse' he came near to describing it as it still looks to-day. Its outside wall—surely the ugliest in Britain—still bears the scars of its story; in two centuries it served as farmyard, embryo-monastery, printing works and almshouse and is now turning into an international shrine.

To take John Henry first, his conversion to Catholicism caused much confusion; as he leased the College, was it now Catholic or Protestant? For a fleeting moment, John Henry thought of staying but his good friend from Oriel, Charles Marriott, offered to take up the lease. Marriott undoubtedly had his friend's interest in mind but there were others who wanted the renegade Vicar out of the village and feared that other papist squatters might arrive.

John Henry loved Littlemore for deep, personal reasons but the College had no hold on him now. He saw it as 'a very rude place' which he was just getting into shape. The College had played its part, was poverty-stricken, with all the furniture secondhand. When his library had been packed, he abandoned an inventory and left Marriott all but a few items which could be taken by a fly. He mourned the garden wall, his covered passage and the door fittings but these could not be taken in a cab.

Charles Marriott moved in at once with his printing presses, found local labour, produced three or four small books of some distinction in the next two years. Worn out by the work, he, then, went back to Oriel and *The Library of the Fathers,* leaving the College to the diocese of Oxford for the help of the poor. The College became an almshouse, administered by the Vicars of Littlemore for just a hundred years.

Dear Mrs Clarke, eighty-eight by her own reckoning, must enter the College story at this point. A Sandford girl, not that long married, Mrs Clarke came to Littlemore in 1927, pushing her eldest daughter—little Eva—in a pram. She had come to tend old Fanny and John, her husband's parents, well over seventy who were sick.

Mrs Clarke and Eva have lived in the College ever since. Her personal memories now cover fifty-six years. To these she may add the reminiscences of her Father-in-Law and old John Clarke was born in Littlemore in 1847, just a year after John Henry Newman left the College for good. Mrs Clarke knows for sure that Dr Newman planted the hornbeam in the garden and that he sat before the fire of an evening with his feet bare.

Mrs Clarke returns again and again to the same conclusions, the first, that Newman's College was painfully austere. She should know after half a life-time walking on bricks. Carpets proved impossible and linoleum slipped about and split. Coconut matting served best but was inclined to smell.

Mrs Clarke often reverts to the almshouse days, every room crowded with adults and children; outside toilets, a common pump; coal fires and candles before the advent of gas. John Henry's covered passage was totally enclosed with bricks and slate to add a kitchen and scullery to each tenement. In return, each tenement lost one of its two windows to give each tenant a front door. Both Mrs Clarke and Eva still speak with horror of rats and mice. Yet they smile to recall the weekly visits to the Vicarage to pay two shillings and sixpence for the rent.

College Almshouse

On January 31st, 1951, the Vicar, accepting the rent, informed them that he was leaving and that they should in future pay their rents at a new address. Mrs Clarke made a note but at that time the Fathers of the Birmingham Oratory meant nothing to her.

The Fathers of Birmingham Oratory knew nothing of Mrs Clarke. Their information stopped with the news that the diocese of Oxford had put the College on the market, the asking price £2,000. They felt the filial urge to acquire the broken-down building where Stanton, Dalgairns, Bowles, St John and other pioneers, now long departed, had started their pilgrimage at the College with the Padre, a century ago. The College was acquired but it took them nine years to decide what to do with it. Some were for selling the site, others suggested a small, resident community, or a gift of the College to the Converts Aid Society to help others in the same quandary as they had known themselves. A fourth and most happy solution was finally adopted, that the College should be restored. Mrs Clarke, Eva and the other inmates should remain as tenants but John Henry's room and Oratory should be available to the public and sacrosanct.

Father Humphrey Crookenden, a perfectionist and an expert, with enthusiasm unbounded, was made Prefect of Littlemore in 1958. An improvement grant was given by the Council and the roof, near to collapse, was tackled first. Next, John Henry's beloved shed was uncovered, windows were refitted and the many front doors in College Lane were swept away. Mrs Clarke and the other residents moved to other quarters in the building as their apartments were restored, one by one. As each flat has now a bathroom and kitchen, the cottages differ slightly from the monastic cells of Newman's day. The number of windows has not changed. With John Henry's great library now in Edgbaston, the original barn which once housed it can never look the same.

What has happened to the tough red bricks about which Mrs Clarke and Eva used to complain? They are still there but Fr Humphrey covered them over with wood in the cottages and tarmac along the shed. You may still see it in one all-important place.

Old Mrs Howse and her family were the last people to occupy John Henry's rooms. Father Humphrey asked them to move further down the passage that he might begin his chief labour of love. In John Henry's room, the rough, worn bricks, cold and uncomfortable, were left exposed. The old brown cupboard in the corner was part of the older building; Mrs Clarke had a similar structure in her almshouse room. Father Humphrey acquired the miniature by Sir William Ross, painted in 1846, the very year that John Henry left the College for good.

The little oratory next door was easily restored for John Henry, in a letter already quoted, set out all the details and, if you remember, it was Bloxam who decided that the draperies should be red. The only addition to the little chapel is John Henry's borrowed writing and reading desk which was used as part of the altar when BI Dominic Barberi offered Mass.

Dear Mrs Clarke still conducts visitors to John Henry's rooms. These now come from all over the world, thoughtful people in their hundreds, drawn by the genius and holiness of the first Vicar of Littlemore, one of the greatest churchmen of all times.

Bernard Basset was born in London in 1909. He was educated at Hodder and Stonyhurst and entered the Jesuit novitiate in 1927. He spent some years as a teacher and in parishes at Bournemouth and the Scilly Isles. He was very popular as a retreat director, preacher and a prolific writer. He wrote at least 10 books of popular spirituality, and a comprehensive history of the early British Jesuits. He found his calling in helping the ordinary laity to better understand and live their faith. In this he was inspired by Newman whom he studied extensively all of his life. For several years he lived at The College and eventually wrote *Newman at Littlemore*. He suffered a heart attack in 1984. As a consequence of diabetes, both his legs were later amputated. But he never lost his great humor and interior strength rooted in a life of prayer. He died in Oxford at Nazareth House in 1988.

Part II

'Dear Mrs Clarke still conducts visitors to John Henry's rooms'. This description of life at The College was true when this booklet was skilfully written by Fr Basset in the nineteen-eighties; but today it is different. Dear Mrs Clarke died in 1987, in the year in which the Spiritual Family *The Work* was entrusted with the care of The College by the Birmingham Oratory. Members of this community guide the visitors to John Henry's rooms today.

The *Spiritual Family The Work*, a family of consecrated life of pontifical right, was founded in 1938 in Belgium by Mother Julia Verhaeghe (1910–1997). Reading a Newman biography and anthology in the early nineteen-sixties, she recognized in him a 'brother of her soul'. Guided by God's providence, the community organized a Newman Symposium, the first ever in Rome, in the Holy Year 1975. It was then, that the co-operation between The Work and the Birmingham Oratory began. When in 1976 the well-known Newman scholar, Fr Stephen Dessain CO, suddenly died, Sr Lutgart Govaert FSO, who had written her doctoral thesis on Newman's Mariology at the Pontifical Gregorian University in Rome, was sent by her Superiors to come to the help of the Oratorians. She began to work as the organizing secretary of *The Friends of Cardinal Newman*, an organization which had been planned by Fr Dessain. Putting his plans into reality, Sr Lutgart lived in Birmingham for several years until others could take over from her. Over these years, the ties of friendship between the two communities grew.

When in 1986 one of the Cottages at The College became vacant, Fr Gregory Winterton, CO, (†2012), the then Provost of the Birmingham Oratory, asked the Superiors of The Work if Sisters could help with the welcome of pilgrims and take a share in the upkeep of The College. Since 1982 Miss Patricia Taylor, a fervent convert and good friend of Fr Basset, has been the Custodian of The College. Fr Winterton's request was granted and the first Sisters arrived in June 1986. Sr Brigitte M. Hoegemann FSO, who would be the leading force in the development of the mission of The Work at Littlemore for many years, arrived in September. In 1987, Miss Taylor († 2006) had to give up the task at the College which she loved with all her heart for health reasons and offered Ambrose Cottage, her house situated next to The College, for sale. Supported by generous benefactors The Work was able to acquire the house making it their home.

The College now

The Society of The Work, a Registered Charity, was established and an International Centre of Newman Friends set up. The Work has co-operated with the Birmingham Oratory in the renovation and maintenance of The College. In 1990, the oratory, which had seen Newman's reception into the Church, became a chapel where the Blessed Sacrament was reserved for the first time on 18th January. A permanent altar was put into the chapel and Newman's reading desk can now be admired in the library.

The Chapel at the College

With the years, the various inhabitants of The College moved out. Dear Eva Clarke, Mrs Clarke's daughter, the last inhabitant from almshouse times, passed away on 2nd July 2005. She had been a quiet presence in The College and good friend of The Sisters. The Work then took on the responsibility for all the Cottages of The College, turning them into Guest Cottages for people interested to spend some days in prayer and study.

Over these years, The Spiritual Family—again with the generous help of many benefactors—has gathered a substantial collection of Newman's writings and Newman-related literature and created a permanent exhibition of Newman memorabilia (prints, paintings, etchings, photographs, sculptures and original letters) in Newman's former library. The collection gives an excellent insight into the life and work of Blessed John Henry Newman.

The specialized Newman library is available for scholars and Newman friends.

The Newman library

Visitors come from all over the world and enjoy the atmosphere of peace and tranquillity. Mass is being celebrated often in Newman's former oratory. Visitors and guests who stay for some days at The College can take part in the prayer life of the Community. A good number of people for whom Newman has been an inspiration and spiritual guide have been received into the Catholic Church in Newman's former oratory. The guest rooms in The College are well used for days of recollection and retreats and restful holidays.

In 1990, The Work organized the first Nightwalk from Oxford to Littlemore on 8th October commemorating Blessed Dominic Barberi's arrival at Littlemore and Newman's request to be received into 'the one fold of the Redeemer'. It has become an annual joint event with the Fathers of the Oxford Oratory. Other events (talks, days of prayer, fundraising events etc.) are organized at other times of the year.

The Night Walk

Newman devotees, who come to Littlemore, can visit Newman's church of St Mary's and St Nicholas, which serves as the Anglican parish church. Newman's memory is still cherished, and visitors may see the memorial plaque in honour of Newman's mother Jemima, the list of benefactors of the church, the baptismal font which Newman brought in from St Mary's in Oxford, and a modern icon depicting Newman as a Cardinal. The parish continues Newman's concern in the care of its people of Littlemore.

Blessed Dominic Barberi, the Catholic parish church, was built at the end of the nineteen-sixties. Visitors can admire a bronze sculpture by Faith Tolkien (1995) showing John Henry Newman asking Blessed Dominic for reception into the Church. The church and hall are used by Newman pilgrims when the premises of The College are too small.

In the village, road names like Cardinal Close, Barberi Close, Newman Road, College Lane are reminders of Newman's stay. St George's in Cowley Road, Littlemore, where Newman lived while overseeing the works at The College, has been restored by a private owner.

Since John Henry Newman's beatification in 2010 by Pope Benedict XVI, a bronze statue by Heather Burnley stands in a corner of the former oratory, now chapel, and invites pilgrims and visitors to put their prayers and intentions trustfully into the hands of Blessed John Henry Newman. John Henry would never have thought that his poor dwelling would be transformed in this way. However, in a hidden but real way he welcomes those who enter The College gate today 'drawn by the genius and holiness of the first Vicar of Littlemore, one of the greatest churchmen of all times', as Fr Basset expressed it.

Bronze statue of Cardinal Newman by Heather Burnley

For further information about visits to The College and so forth please consult www.newmanfriendsinternational.org.

APPENDIX

Three letters of John Henry Newman connected with Littlemore

A MOST VALUABLE SOURCE for those who are interested to know even more about Newman's life at Littlemore are his Letters and Diaries (*The Letters and Diaries of John Henry Newman*, Edited by Charles Stephen Dessain and others in 32 Volumes, Oxford University Press, 1961—2008) and in particular Volumes II to XI. The collection of Newman memorabilia at The College in Littlemore contains a few of these letters of which three are given here as an example and as a 'little taster':

Letter to his sister Jemima Mozley, 22nd March 1845[1]

Newman had disclosed to his sister Jemima in March 1845 that he was contemplating leaving the Anglican Church. This occasioned a painful exchange of letters between them. John Henry tried to explain his motives, but she found them incomprehensible. She wrote to him again on Good Friday 1845 and he answered the next day, Holy Saturday.

Despite of his pain, he does not forget to wish his sister God's blessing and he hopes that she will visit him at Littlemore with her husband. He mentions an altar cloth in Littlemore church. It had been made by Jemima herself and it was their pride and joy. The postscript of the letter speaks about Newman's aunt Elizabeth. He owed to her part of his early religious instruction and felt very close to

---

[1]   *The Letters and Diaries of John Henry Newman* X (Oxford: OUP, 2006), p. 606f.

her. It hurts him, that she was unsettled by the rumour (expressed in some newspapers) that he wants to enter the Catholic Church. However, he feels he must follow the voice of his conscience, convinced that his eternal salvation depends on it.

Easter Eve, March 22/45

My dear Jemima,

I have received your very kind letter on this day, the most soothing and peaceful in the whole year—the true Sabbath, or day of rest.

I write you a line because I am sorry to see I have not guarded against your mistaking me in one point. When I said 'fancy the perplexity of my being right', I did not mean 'fancy your being wrong'. Surely I have enough to do just now to look to myself—and it was in answer to your saying I was mistaken that I wrote, not dreaming of others. You do agree with me in feeling that this is a case where every one must stand by himself—As you are obliged to form your own judgment, so you must let me form mine, and that is all I meant to say; and as it does not come into my mind to take the responsibility of judging you, so you must not, as you do not wish, judge me.

It is indeed a great perplexity how what is a rule for me is not a rule for another—as if there were two truths—but, alas, any how we are in the state of perplexity—and we must submit to what is at present a sort of mystery.

I could not get myself to read that portion of your letter which was a defence of yourself, for, believe me, I had no intention whatever of attacking you.

May all good come down upon you, and all about you at this blessed time—I quite long to see you, but that is impossible, for I have so many things to do. I live in hope that you and John will pass through Oxford in your way some whither—do come and see us once again. The Altar Cloth will be put on tomorrow for the <u>sixth</u> year!

I am setting to read all my writings, Sermons and Lectures—by way of throwing myself into my old thoughts and feelings—and seeing what will come of it.

What you said of Aunt even before, led me to hope perhaps she suspects more than she chose to say. I don't like to lay out plans for myself, but I suppose I should publish something before any thing happened. Thus there would be two things, first my weighing my feelings up and then a publication. I can't help trusting that when I act I shall be much happier, both because the very fact of acting presupposes that my mind is made up—and next because doubt and suspence are so very depressing. I do trust I am undergoing the chief pain <u>before</u> I take any step—Also I trust that, much pain as you and others must feel, yet when it is over, you will find it less than you expect, and that things altogether will be more tolerable.

Surely good must come of all acts done from a sense of duty—and I certainly trust that the time I am taking before acting will be graciously used by God's Mercy to show me, if my conscience is erroneous.

Evr Yrs affly J H N

P.S.: I wish you would think <u>under what form</u>, and with <u>what reasons</u> the step could be most intelligibly told to Aunt. I mean how she would most be reconciled to it—whether, e.g. it should be put to her on public grounds, the censures, so many Bishops have discoursed against me etc. But I

suppose it is best to say the plain reason that I find
it necessary for my salvation.

Letter to his sister Jemima Mozley, 8th October 1845[2] (LD XI, 8f.)

Of the some thirty letters which Newman wrote between
seventh and ninth of October 1845 informing friends
about his decision to enter the Catholic Church, this might
be the one which caused himself most pain to write. The
news he expressed would not be a surprise to Jemima, but
it would still be very difficult for her to accept. Although
Jemima failed to understand his motives, she kept in touch
with her brother throughout her life and they frequently
corresponded. His other sister Harriett, had broken off
relations with her brother two or three years earlier
because she disliked his religious development and they
were never restored.

Littlemore. Oct. 8. 1845

My dear Jemima,

I must tell you, what will pain you greatly, but I will
make it as short as you would wish me to do.

This night Father Dominic the Passionist, sleeps
here. He does not know of my intention, but I shall
ask him to receive me into what I believe to be the
One Fold of the Redeemer. This will not go, till all
is over.

Every Yours affectly

John H Newman

---

2 *The Letters and Diaries of John Henry Newman* XI (Oxford:
OUP, 1961), p. 8f.

Letter to Revd George William Huntingford, 17th June 1868[3]

The Revd George Huntingford was Vicar of Littlemore from 1851 to 1872. He recognized Newman standing at the lych gate on 16th June 1868. Newman had come with Ambrose St John by train from Birmingham. He spent the whole day at Littlemore and found in it great pleasure. It was his first visit to Littlemore since his departure on 21st February 1846. He met various people, among them the Revd George Huntingford. The volume sent to Mrs Huntingford is the edition of some of his poems *Verses on Various Occasions*. The volume forms part of the exhibition at The College.

The Oratory Birmingham June 17. 1868

My dear Mr Huntingford,

I was so unready yesterday that I fear I did not acknowledge properly Mrs Huntingford's kindness in asking me to luncheon.

By way of setting myself right, will you ask her to accept from me a small volume which I send by this post.

Thanking you for your various civilities, which were one chief feature in the happy hours I passed yesterday at Littlemore.

I am, My dear Mr Huntingford Very truly Yours

John Henry Newman

The Revd G. W. Huntingford

---

[3] *The Letters and Diaries of John Henry Newman* XI (Oxford: OUP, 1973), p. 88.

CPSIA information can be obtained
at www.ICGtesting.com
Printed in the USA
LVHW022155150920
666084LV00003B/616

9 780852 449424